MW00461335

Praise for

THE WORK IS THE WORK

"Brian is always one of my first calls when I'm dealing with a challenge or need strategic insight. On a wide range of issues, constituencies, and campaigns, Brian is quite simply one of the most effective, impactful, and thoughtful leaders I know. With this book, *The Work Is the Work*, so many others can now also access his thoughtful and creative leadership style and reflections. Whether you are considering activism for the very first time, are a veteran who wants to take their leadership to the next level, or simply want to be a better human, this book is for you. The lessons in *The Work Is the Work* are timeless and are needed now more than ever."

—**Meg Ansara**, cofounder, Organizing
Corps 2020

"*The Work Is the Work* is for anyone who wants to be good at what they do—be it nonprofit, for-profit, or just being a good human. Attacking systemic and structural challenges like civil rights, racism, criminal justice reform, or gender-based violence is a long, difficult, and at times lonely road when your passion and values are met with resistance to change. The easy-to-digest stories and personal anecdotes give you your own friend in the struggle, reminding you at every page that you aren't alone. While the work of social change may feel never-ending, the fight to make this world a better place begins with a deep-seated belief that all of us have the potential to change the world—right from where we are."

—**Toi Hutchinson**, former Illinois State Senator

"In *The Work is the Work: Letters to a Future Activist*, Brian lays out an intimate and urgent guide for LGBTQ+ activism, informed by twenty-five years of struggle in the fight for social, racial, and economic justice. As the LGBTQ+ community confronts a dire state of emergency, Brian's compelling insights function as both a clarion call to action and a strategic blueprint for structural change."

—**Kelley Robinson**, president, Human Rights Campaign

"Brian Johnson is a compelling storyteller and a gifted writer. Through a combination of humor, wisdom, and his generously shared personal stories, Brian creates a guidebook for advocacy and life that can benefit anyone. *The Work Is the Work* is a must-read."

—**Imani Rupert-Gordon**, executive director, National Center for Lesbian Rights

"Brian is a long-time friend and mentor who has had a tremendous impact on me and my work over the years. Now, with *The Work Is the Work*, more activists can be influenced by his knowledge and experience, just as I've been and continue to be. As a new generation rises up and prepares to lead in our statehouses, Congress, and other areas of power, it is vital that we provide them with the necessary tools and mentorship so they may continue to advance the fight for justice against gun extremists, white supremacists, and others who threaten progress. This book is a must-have for anyone who is ready to roll up their sleeves and make a real difference in the world."

—**Kathleen Sances**, president and CEO, Gun Violence Prevention PAC IL (G-PAC)

"Brian delivers keen insights and strategies through stories that illuminate and inspire. His lessons are rooted in years of experience and reflect his deep love for community. I've gotten to see Brian in action, and I'm thrilled that his book, *The Work Is the Work*, will make his accessible and easy-to-digest advice available to newcomers and veterans alike."

—**Nadine Smith**, Executive Director, Equality Florida and *TIME* 100 Honoree (2022)

"A profoundly raw, honest, and wise journey! In *The Work Is the Work: Letters to a Future Activist*, Brian Johnson offers invaluable wisdom and insights for all change agents. Drawing from a lifetime of experience in social justice, from education reform to human rights, Johnson provides a roadmap for navigating the complexities of embarking on social justice work, as well as the fears we need to face and the hope we must hold on to along that journey. Deftly navigating from Gita to Miley Cyrus, *The Work Is the Work* lays out tangible strategies and a clear call to action. A must-read for anyone looking for inspiration, committed to making a difference in their community, or creating a more equitable society, this book is a beacon of hope, reminding young activists that even in the darkest moments, there are always hands reaching out to guide us forward. Prepare for a transformative reading experience where practical wisdom meets passion, fostering personal growth and societal impact."

—**Dr. Kathleen St. Louis-Caliento**, president and CEO, Cara Collective

"For anyone responding to the call to effect change, *The Work Is the Work* will light the way and ease the path."

—**Brianna Twofoot**, national reproductive rights organizer

"Brian has had a tremendous impact over the years. He brings life to stories in accessible and inspiring ways. To be able to learn from Brian's decades-long work in advocacy and social justice is a treat."

—**Brady Walkinshaw**, CEO, Earth Alliance

The Work Is the Work

BRIAN C. JOHNSON

THE WORK IS THE WORK

LETTERS TO A FUTURE ACTIVIST

Broadleaf Books
Minneapolis

Library of Congress Cataloging-in-Publication Data

Names: Johnson, Brian C. (CEO of Equality Illinois), author.
Title: The work is the work : letters to a future activist / Brian C.
    Johnson.
Description: Minneapolis : Broadleaf Books, 2024.
Identifiers: LCCN 2023039832 (print) | LCCN 2023039833 (ebook) |
    ISBN 9781506493374 (hardcover) | ISBN 9781506493381 (ebook)
Subjects: LCSH: Activism. | Social action. | Social justice.
Classification: LCC HN18.3 .J657 2024 (print) | LCC HN18.3
    (ebook) | DDC 361.2—dc23/eng/20231102
LC record available at https://lccn.loc.gov/2023039832
LC ebook record available at https://lccn.loc.gov/2023039833

Cover design: Angie Chiu
Cover image: shutterstock_1519277591.eps/
shutterstock_1996308668.eps

Print ISBN: 978-1-5064-9337-4
eBook ISBN: 978-1-5064-9338-1

To my Josephine, may you see your Papa's love for you in these pages.

Contents

1

Grace

Let me start by telling you the story of Wanjiru Kibera, who stood alone in the darkness on a mountainside, struggling to breathe.

She had begun the journey as part of a high school class trip to climb Point Lenana, the third-highest peak on Mount Kenya, the sacred mountain of the country that shares its name. An asthma sufferer who was not particularly athletic, she had begun the nighttime journey on the trail to the peak with her classmates. Soon, though, she lagged behind her most active peers while staying ahead of her least fit peers. She was alone in the darkness when an asthma attack gripped her.

Sitting down on the path, afraid and dirty, she worked for each breath. After some time, a guide from a separate group came along the path with his charge. He stopped and asked Wanjiru what had brought her there. Through tears and short breaths, she told her story.

"Don't worry," he soothed, "we'll go together, and I will help you up."

Extending a hand, the guide helped Wanjiru to her feet, and the three of them—guide, charge, and Wanjiru—worked their way along the night path. Just as the sun began to rise, Wanjiru reached the top and saw her classmates. They welcomed her into their huddle as they watched day break across the savannah.

Much later, through tears, Wanjiru told this story to a live audience as part of The Moth storytelling project. She said the high school administrators had planned the trip up Mount Kenya to teach "endurance and patience and courage" leading into final exams. But the lesson Wanjiru learned was not about how to get through exams or bring about success. What she learned was that in life, there will be darkness and aloneness and fear and struggle. But that people often come along to hold your hand and help you move forward.

So she now encourages others to tell their own stories—ones that reveal different and sometimes unexpected wisdom.

"Tell the story of the mountains you climb," she implores us, "because your words can become a survival guide in someone else's book."

That is what this book is. These are my field notes, collected over decades in social justice work. I am old enough to have stumbled my way onto some truths about the work. What you hold in your hands is a gathering of the wisdom I have scribbled down and stashed away over the years, collected as a student of religion at an East Coast university, a public school teacher in Louisiana, a political candidate in Los Angeles, and a civil rights leader in Chicago. There is much I do not know and cannot teach you. To learn how to write the smartest law or argue calmly in front of great judges, you'll have to turn elsewhere. To understand how to communicate with wit and precision on social media, you'll have to find other models. But what I can teach you is how to plow through the work of taking care of your community.

If you haven't already, one day soon you will look beyond your home to the world and confront its tragedies, wounds, and pain. You may want to help heal this world. When you do, I hope these assembled notes may serve as a survival guide for you—warnings to avoid the traps that have ensnared me, insight from the sages who have walked before me and you, maybe even a map to help you navigate your way.

I share these notes from the field so that, one day, as you trudge along your own rocky path of making your community better, you might be able to turn to a page here or there and find some guidance for the rough terrain. If nothing else, I hope that in these pages you at least see how one activist from one generation cares for you and your journey ahead.

In sharing what I have learned, let me first tell you a bit more about what brings me here, what roles I have played in my life that have earned me these insights. I share this with you so you know the context and my intent. I share this so you may more fully know all my biases and prejudices. I hope that understanding all of this will help you choose what to take from me and what to leave on the page. For not all my learnings will speak to you. I know not all of one generation's lessons are right for the next.

I come to you here in these pages first as a student.

As a teenager, I left my parents' suburban Virginia home and showed up like a stranger at my elite eastern university. Stepping onto that campus was like stepping into another country, a pristine and storied country but one where I knew none of the customs or the language or the people.

I was uncertain about so much in those early days, including what I should study. Initially, I was drawn to politics or policy or history—majors that spoke to my interest in the world around me. But then something almost magical happened. Immersed in a campus culture that valued curiosity, I was encouraged to dabble. The rich diversity of classes and guest lectures, the range of artistic endeavors and new sports all inspired me to try different things on. This was so far from the norm-gravitating pull of my high school days, and I loved it.

So when I stumbled on the electric courses being taught by fascinating professors in the small religion department, I was riveted. There was philosopher Jeff Stout, whose wiry frame, shorn hair, and round glasses gave him the look of a contemplative marathon runner. There was Buzzy Teiser, who taught courses on Buddhism and whose funny aging-hippie persona masked an intense brilliance. There was Al Raboteau, who studied African American religious history and taught his students with a measured speaking cadence and electrifying white hair bursting in every direction. There was something magical about being surrounded by Gothic buildings, taught by these quirky professors, and steeped in these mystical courses.

But the class that grabbed ahold of me the most tightly was Spiritual Biography and Autobiography with the gnostic Christian scholar Elaine Pagels. Every week she introduced us to sages like Annie Dillard, Ramakrishna, and Malcolm X. I got to spend each week trying to understand how a different deep thinker made sense of the world around them. I reveled in the mysticism these spiritual leaders uncovered. I would lie on my bed in my hundred-square-foot room and get lost in readings that seemed significant and magical, so different from the everyday struggles of a twenty-year-old college sophomore.

Professor Pagels and her course gifted me with the start of a lifelong passion for learning from wise spiritual thinkers across many cultures and traditions. What started as a random grabbing at whatever books or talks inspired me in the moment eventually gave way to a more deliberate practice. I now keep the practice, waking up early most mornings to start my day with quiet reading. And more often than not, this reading is spiritual in form: Brennan Manning, Greg Boyle, Howard Thurman, Robin Wall Kimmerer, Ross Gay, Henri Nouwen, and Rabbi Abraham Joshua Heschel.

Over the years, I have collected so much of the wisdom of these voices in my notebook, in the margins of their books, in my own memory. I mention them because you will see their teachings and the teachings of so many others peppered throughout these pages.

I come to you also as a witness.

When I was a child, my father served in the army. Our life was in constant motion, moving to a new town only to uproot ourselves a year later. I lived in eleven different homes before I was fourteen years old. As a result, I spent much of my childhood on the outside looking in, trying to make sense of who this new group of people was—studying how they spoke, which sports they followed, how they played, how they structured themselves socially. Sometimes I picked it up quickly. Often I did not. But trying to make sense of ever-changing communities forged in me a deep curiosity for the ever-changing cast of people around me.

As my career brought me to many places and many roles, it also introduced me to a wide range of people having tremendous impact on their communities. By studying those around me, I have picked up countless insights from seeing how this diverse cross section of peers and mentors has led. I have watched a social entrepreneur grow a small organization stemming from the seed of a great idea into a national powerhouse. I have watched parent organizers and teacher leaders transform the communities in which they lived and worked. I have followed the career advice given to me humbly by Fortune 500 CEOs and federal judges. One of the greatest gifts in my life has been the opportunity to come so close to many profound community leaders and to be granted the humility and curiosity to learn from them.

But there is another form of witness I bear: witness across difference.

Beneath the surface-level outsiderness of my childhood grew a deeper outsiderness, one that both frightened and shamed me. The emerging secret of being gay whispered in my ears that I was not only different but deserved to be different; I not only didn't belong but I deserved not to belong. If you knew the loving warmth of my home today, it would seem hard to fathom how isolating the threat of being gay was. But as a teen, I saw no gay role models—in politics, on TV, or in stories. And our church taught me I was sinful and worthy only of rejection. So I was adrift in my differentness, lost in my shame.

How I moved past this is a longer story for another time. I found my voice and my pride. I found my husband and my daughter. But this early experience of standing apart from my community and feeling like I deserved it taught me how to look not only with curiosity but with a keen eye for how power exudes and how power excludes.

Serving as a witness with an eye toward understanding how power can harm sharpens one's focus. Ask the kid bullied on the playground or the Black man pulled over by the police.

And true, I haven't always been on the ebbing side of power. True, I have lived as a gay man in towns rife with homophobia where I had few legal protections. I have moved through halls of power where my identity was a barely concealed joke. But other times I was in work, where I brought with me all the social power of my maleness or my whiteness. I was, after all, a white teacher in a Black community. I led organizations as a cis man with an elite degree. But living so much of my life conscious of the risks around me has sharpened my awareness of power differentials and the threats they pose.

So it is this eye, one of constant outsiderness—sometimes with power, sometimes without—that honed my awareness to a finer point. For learning from those around me was not just a source of wisdom; it was also sometimes a requirement for survival. In classrooms and boardrooms and backrooms where deals are struck, I have watched and learned and took it all in.

Finally, I come to you as a practitioner.

I have stood in front of twenty-five five-year-olds as a first-grade teacher on the north side of Baton Rouge. I have run a public school network in the heart of Hollywood that served a student community that mirrored the wild and vibrant diversity of the city. I have hired teams of community organizers working with teachers in communities ranging from Atlanta to New York, from Houston to the Pine Ridge Reservation of South Dakota. I have built coalitions with stakeholders throughout Illinois to push legislators and governors to make our state one of the most queer-affirming states in the country.

I have raised money, built power, grown teams, and changed laws. I have lost a campaign, failed as a team leader, missed fundraising goals, and been bested on legislative floors. In short, I have learned through a few wins and many losses in communities across this country and in numerous lines of work.

Student. Witness. Practitioner. These are the sources of my insight.

This book is the resulting collection of wisdom I have picked up along the way. It is the prayers, the texts, the parables that have steadied my feet and lightened my emotional load in this work. Even as I know that each tool of wisdom is far more powerful than my ability to wield it, I hope that by sharing them, you can use them more gracefully and effectively than I have.

The work. You deserve to know what I mean when I use that heavy and broad word.

If you haven't already, you will turn to the world one day and ask what it demands of you. You will look out on your community and want it to be better. I write this, then, as a letter to you as you begin to roll up your sleeves and engage in the hard labor of making your world a better place.

Maybe you will be a teacher who wakes up before the sun rises to drive the lonely predawn route to school and bring wisdom and love to kids who need it. Maybe you will be a doctor who misses tucking in your own children at night because you must stay with your patients. Maybe you will be a writer for justice who sits alone for hours, wrestling with your inner demons and weaknesses to whittle away something that might galvanize action.

But this book is also for those for whom *the work* is not your full-time job. For when you chair the Parent Teacher Association (PTA), ending long days in the office with meetings to support the next school fundraiser or defend a widened curriculum. For when you are a volunteer who spends your Saturday afternoons at the food bank. For when you rush between your own children's soccer practices and dance lessons to stop by the nursing home to sit quietly with your father, who remembers you less frequently with every visit.

While I don't know which way your work will unfold, I do know that the work itself will always call to you. Maybe you are a woman in a world that will seek to limit your power and quiet your voice. Maybe you live with a disability in a world that builds its public spaces to a norm that doesn't fit you. Maybe you are a person of color moving in a society that centers whiteness above all else. Maybe you are queer in a world where self-serving politicians seek to erase you from classrooms and arrest parents who care for their trans children. Maybe you hold multiple of these and other identities thriving—or working to thrive—in a country whose default is not to honor your dignity.

The world is not easy for those of us whose love and power and beauty break the mold. That is where the work stems from.

So when I say *the work*, I mean the sacred, mundane, messy, tiring slog of committing to make the lives of the people around you better every day or every week. This, then, is for you in whatever form your work takes, whether you are a revolutionary, a reformer, or an everyday do-gooder. The work will be heavy. It always is. I hope these notes help make carrying the load a little easier.

Yet, as I sit down to write this book, I fend off the gnawing fear of you finding me out as an impostor, projecting myself as wise when I know I am not. What I am, though, is a collector of wisdom. I pick up pieces of truth and insight the way you collect seashells on the beach. I have stuffed my pockets with these seashells. I sometimes have had the foresight to take them out, look at them, and live into them. "Oh, I remember this one," I'll marvel. "It is so beautiful, and yet I forgot all about it." Each time, I promise to keep *this* insight at the top of my mind, even knowing that I will likely fail.

And I practice my failings every day. Like you, like all of us, I live with my poor decisions and stumble along with my weaknesses. I drink more than I should. I can be selfish in my marriage and short with my daughter. I wrestle with bouts of envy and resentment. I descend into vitriol and self-righteous arguments with others in my mind. I allow uncertainty to drive anxiety. I fight the urge to hoard resources to protect against the fear of future loss.

I worry that my everyday weaknesses juxtaposed against the wisdom in this book may make me come off like a hypocrite. What if you read this book and then see me one day leaning on my horn at a driver who cut me off or condescending in snippy frustration to the agent at the airline check-in counter? What if you meet someone in my life I have hurt, and they tell you of it?

A while back, while living in Los Angeles before I met my husband, I went on a few dates with an aspiring television writer. He was brooding and dazzling. God, he was handsome. But his muted charisma came from something beyond his looks. He was quiet with a powerful focused gaze.

Inevitably we talked about our coming-out stories, this ritual being a rite of passage on early dates among gay men. On our third date we sat in a quiet Italian restaurant caught in the bustle of Santa Monica Boulevard in West Hollywood, where he told me he came from a devoutly evangelical family. He shared their faith. His coming-out was tough and fraught with tension with his parents—the tension that holds the space among a loving family, an unbending faith, and an immutable self. I asked if they had accepted him.

At this, he paused. Slowly he shared that he had moved toward his family as far as he could without denying who he was. And his family had moved toward him as far as they could without denying their faith. And the gap, he said, would have to be covered by grace.

The gap would have to be covered by grace.

I had always thought of grace as this powerful metaphysical force that rescues sinners, imbues prophets with wisdom, and performs miracles. But in that moment, I realized another more concrete way to understand grace: that which covers the gap. The gap between how far we can come on our own and where we need to be. When the distance is great, maybe that grace is powerful. But when that distance is narrow, that grace can serve as the gentle bridges that bind us to our better selves and to each other.

This book is my own offering and my own prayer for grace. I present to you the wisdom I have collected and the vulnerabilities that have earned me that wisdom. I share with you a life in the making, not complete. I offer you learnings still being worked out and practices still being honed. And my hope is that as you read this, you offer me an inch more grace than I may deserve. That whatever my imperfections, you'll see the greater truth that lies underneath.

I know I move through the world bruised and imperfect. But I still have these stones of wisdom in my pocket, some rubbed glossy from use. It seems wrong to hoard them because of my selfish fears. So I'm humbly sharing them with you. I tell you their stories, how they came to me, and how I have used them. And if you take even a few stones from this collection and pocket them and draw power from them on your journey, then I am happy. Even if you return them all to the page, unused and untouched, I am simply grateful you took the time with my insights and my stories. What a blessing that is for an activist who loves his community and hungers for justice.

2

Leap

The other day my daughter was napping upstairs, and I was collapsed on the couch scrolling through social media on my phone. At some point, I came across a fifteen-minute documentary showcasing people standing on the edge of a diving platform nearly four stories tall. None of these people had ever been on a diving platform so high. I watched, recognizing the fear in these novice divers' body language. The stepping back and forth. The tipping one's head forward just a bit to see how high up they were.

Seeing these people peer out thirty feet up made my heart race.

But what amazed me in the end was not just how familiar their reactions were to me. What amazed me was how many of them jumped. Against their mind's racing fears and their body's desperate desire to stay rooted in place, most of them took the plunge. We are all so much braver than we know.

We are all called to do something.

Sometimes this calling will take the form of a nagging desire to see change in your community or in the world. This is the calling that will lap at your daydreams and will capture your idle thoughts. This is where your mind will regularly wander when you are driving, or on a run, or in the shower. When I want to uncover what dreams are eating at someone, I might ask, "If you had a magic wand and could improve people's lives within a five-mile radius of where you sit right now, what would you change?" Those harboring an itch for something different usually have a pretty ready answer.

For some, this calling will take the form of a frustration you can't quite let go of. When you come across a news story about it, it will make your blood boil. When it comes up in conversation, you won't be able to stop yourself from ranting. Like a cut in your mouth, you will tongue at it obsessively. When I ask someone, "Tell me about a time you've been angry in the past few months," those cultivating a relentless ire about something are also quick to reply.

Sometimes these drives that grab ahold of us are incredibly specific. The schools I ran in Los Angeles were founded by parents who wanted a high-performing, racially and socioeconomically diverse public school for their children. The fact that one didn't exist in their community ate at them until they started to build their own such school in the neighborhood.

More often, though, these drives are nebulous. I wrote my first book on economic inequality in America, proposing a partial solution I called a *citizen dividend*. But for two years before I even cracked open a laptop and wrote a single sentence, I stewed on economic inequality. I didn't even have a clear understanding of what was driving me or why. I was just deeply appalled by this inequality and kept devouring every news article, book, and scholarly paper I could on the subject.

Here is what I have learned about these yearnings over the years.

Listen to what calls you. In my own life and in the work of helping others to bring about the change they want in the world, I have understood that the calling holds real truth and power. There are times when it may be faint and times when it may be loud. It may be fuzzy, or it may be crystal clear. But there is something to that calling.

Elizabeth Gilbert tells us Zen Buddhists teach about the two forces that transform an acorn into a tree: the acorn itself, "which holds all the promise and potential," and the future tree, "which wants so badly to exist that it pulls the acorn into being." Our longings—or our desires and frustrations—have in them the stuff of the acorn and the future tree. They hold our unique talents and life experiences as well as the energy of our future selves and future worlds that want so much to be brought forth.

Maybe another way to see what you are called to, as theologian Frederick Buechner writes, "is the place where your deep gladness and the world's deep hunger meet." Your job will be to find the overlap. After all, the first call of *the work* is seeking to understand the world's—and our community's—great needs. But we must also listen to what sings to our talents and interests. If we only heed the world's needs and ignore our drive, we may be tempted to work on something we are not best positioned to impact. In that way, the best of our talents and skills are wasted. Conversely, if we only listen to our wants and drives with little care for what the world needs, we become ego-driven imps doing little to make the world better, maybe even making it worse off in our drive to satisfy our yearnings.

For Buechner, our calling sits at the space where our unique desires and the world's deep needs meet. Your job then will be to suss this out. To turn to the world with curiosity and openness. And to honor the hopes and frustrations and anger you hold in yourself. Working to discern this longing is frightening as all get-out. You might fear uncovering what lurks deep inside you. In the search for our calling, we are all bound to come across the maelstrom of ego and distraction. In the lore of shipwrecks, we find legends of raiders who used false lights posing as lighthouses to lure ships to crash on rocks, exposing their bounty to the scavenge. What if we follow one of these false lights?

But a true lighthouse is the pull you will feel to do work even if you imagine few people may notice. The guiding beacon you can trust shines forth from the place where your mind dreams of actually doing the job, not from the place of fantasies for title or praise. I think some of the scariest people I have met are those who want to *be* something more than they want to *do* something. A lot of people scramble for titles, striving to become someone deemed important instead of setting about the inglorious labor of pulling their communities together toward a common vision. By contrast, I imagine the truest singers are those buoyed by the thought of singing, even after the lights have faded and the crowds have turned their backs.

Our job is to sift through it all. The noise and the mess and the siren songs. To listen patiently. To search persistently. To uncover what nuggets are left when the shine of prospective praise and fame is gone.

But there is another reason that discerning your calling may frighten you. You may actually find what you are looking for. And the calling you find may be a rocky, daunting path full of long days and sleepless nights, public ridicule and extended bouts of loneliness. Or, to be fair, the calling you find may also be a path full of meaning and rich experiences. Most likely, the calling will lead you to both deep valleys and high mountaintops. But the recognition that what you find may require risk and sacrifice beyond what you have ever known may be enough to make you wary of starting the search.

Do it anyway.

Maybe in reading this book, you are at the beginning of this process and are worried about what you might find. Maybe you have found your calling and are afraid to embrace it. Maybe you are in the middle of these steps or past it all and starting again. Life is not linear, after all.

Somehow, someway, you will be on the edge of the platform. Like those first-time divers, you will sense you are on the precipice staring down a mighty drop. You can climb down and lumber back to the world of the known. Or you can step off the edge. Only you will know whether it is right to jump or when. But let me share three hard-earned tools that have given me the courage to take the leap.

Give Yourself Permission to Fail

Whatever your work is, you will be bad at it. Full stop. You will probably not be bad at it forever. Keep at it, and you will likely get pretty good at it. But at least in the beginning, and sometimes in the middle, and occasionally even at the end, you will be bad at it.

Many of us feel inspired by the speeches and stories and heroic deeds of the great champions. We want to do the work because we have seen others go before us and make a real difference. And then we set out on the path— or imagine setting out on the path—and realize we are just not that good at it. The first couple of times, or couple hundred times, that we give a little speech or ask someone to donate or plan some event, it kinda sucks. We are awkward and ineloquent, and people we don't know that well respond to that or, more accurately, don't respond at all. Some of us don't even make it out the gate. We know how bad we will be in those first few attempts and don't even try.

The author Anne Lamott teaches us that "perfectionism is the voice of the oppressor." Perfectionism wants you to believe that only the Great Ones—the Holy, the Chosen Prophets, the Celebrated Leaders—do the work. So don't get started, Perfectionism whispers, until you are already that good. This is a load of shit. The deep desire to be great and the recognition that we will fall short stop too many potentially great community leaders—and artists and writers—from ever moving forward.

But here's the secret: everyone experiences that. The only way through it is through it.

Do the work. Get better. Maybe you'll never be world-class. But you'll get better, a lot better.

Even if we stick with it—hone our skills and improve our craft—we may still fail. Dolly Parton is one of the greatest songwriters of all time. As of this writing, 109 of her songs have been on the Billboard charts. But here's the deal. Dolly Parton estimates she has written over five thousand songs in her life. This means 97 percent of the songs Dolly wrote never cracked a chart.

The world lionizes the winners. But behind every winner are scores of people just as good, or better, who did not win. The time was not right for them or their talents to have an outsized impact. I think Barack Obama is one of the most remarkable political leaders of my time. But I have also traveled the country to know there are many more Obamas out there who just didn't rise to the level of prominence that he did. Obama is a gifted orator, but I have seen a teacher in Denver and a poet in Washington, DC, who would run circles around him. Obama is a brilliant scholar, but I have sat in classrooms and read books by even more gifted scholars. Obama is skilled at pulling together teams of great leaders all working together for the good of the country, but I have seen school principals in Los Angeles and executives in New Jersey able to corral the passions and talents of exemplary individuals into similarly stellar teams.

But Obama's unique blend of skills and life experiences was the right fit for the country at the time he was elected. There were many ways in which he may not have made it. Had he won his congressional race in 2000, he might not have run for US Senate in 2004. Had his chief opponent for that Senate race not been caught up in a late-in-campaign sex scandal, Obama may not have won that race. Had the economy not tanked under Republican leadership in the weeks prior to the 2008 election, he may not have been elected president. And if these "what ifs" are real, imagine how many similarly talented leaders we don't know of because the whims of chance did not raise them up to our vision. But Obama's success wasn't just about talent and luck. He was bold enough to put himself out there so that when the currents of history switched in his direction, he was ready to surf them to shore.

The Jesuit priest who works with former gang members in East LA, Father Greg Boyle, says that "anything worth doing is worth failing at." So write that "shitty first draft," as Anne Lamott says. Give that awkward speech. Run for that elected office where you see a path to victory, even if it is obscured and narrow. Put that plan for a better workplace forward, even if others tear it apart at first. In short, give yourself permission to fail. Only when you free yourself from the shackles of the need to be great, will you be able to run headlong into what you are truly destined to do.

Accept Fear

I was an anxious kid. I remember having a pit in my stomach on the way to school every morning in second grade. I can still feel the churning pull of my stomach and the tension spreading out across my chest when I think of my third-grade trips to speech therapy or my history project in the fifth grade.

Only as I got older did I realize that my anxiety was not uniquely borne in me. My mom is an anxious person. Her sister, my aunt Barbara, is an anxious person. I didn't know my great-grandparents well, but my hunch is they were probably anxious people. The constant gnawing of anxiety runs in my family the way curly hair and athletic ability run in others. Fear—the acute distress about potential disaster—has been a smaller presence in my life. But its close cousin anxiety—the constant nagging worry about future failures or potential struggles—has been a lifelong companion. From anxiety's near-constant presence in my life, I have learned two intertwined lessons.

First, something clicked for me when I understood that anxiety and fear are normal and appropriate responses to uncertainty. I am not an anthropologist or a human evolutionary biologist, but I imagine the creative ability to imagine the worst was very productive for early humans. It allowed us to build shelter and protect our young. Looking into the future and imaging failure or horrors befalling us is a totally normal and rational response to uncertainty, especially when looking into a future we care about—a future bound up with our relationships with others, the impact of our work, the health of our communities, and the security of our families. I know this all too well. My worry about the horrors that may befall my daughter and my husband and the LGBTQ+ community I work for is a deeply uncomfortable but rational and reasonable response to not knowing.

Second, anxiety is only anxiety. Fear is only fear. They are not oracular signs that whatever concern tugs at you is right and true. When I get anxious, I get anxious about the fact that I am anxious. I am worried, I used to tell myself, because I am not talented or sufficiently confident to succeed. If I had what it takes to succeed after all, I wouldn't be so worried. Seeing this down on paper, you can probably tell right away how circular and nonsensical this is. Anxiety is merely a conditioned response to uncertainty, not a source of divination. But in the moment, the presence of anxiety seems like a surefire sign that I am deficient in all the important ways.

Put together, fear is normal, and anxiety isn't predictive. They are merely drunken, blustering bullies bumping into the more fragile inhabitants of our minds—confidence and serenity and drive—threatening to topple them. In doing the work, in chasing after big and bold ideas, we'll never get rid of fear and anxiety entirely. So we can cower at their noisy threats of violence, or we can invite them in, give them some water, and embrace them. Make room for them but set clear boundaries. They can have a seat on the comfortable couch on the edge of one's mind and a spot in the guestroom. But they cannot take over our home and threaten the fragile things in it we hold dear. When they get out of line, speak to them lovingly and firmly and put them right back in their place in the corner. When we need the help of professionals or of medication to manage them, we seek them out confident in our dignity in doing so. But for many of us, we can follow Elizabeth Gilbert's lead when she tells her anxiety,

"You're allowed to have a seat, and you're allowed to have a voice, but you are not allowed to have a vote." In fact, fear is what makes us brave. Think of the divers. Or of Noreen Riols, who trained as a British spy during World War II working with "secret agents on special missions." In this work, she came to know many agents on the cusp of being shipped out on dangerous assignments; assignments in which their chances of returning alive stood at fifty-fifty. These agents confided in her, shared their fears. They feared "torture and . . . death." They worried about abandoning their wives and children. After meeting many of these agents and sharing many of their confidences, she learned that "brave [people] are always afraid."

Without fear and the anxiety that grows from it, we would hover somewhere between idiocy and sociopathy. Fear is rooted in our deep love of ourselves and those we care about. We don't want harm or pain to befall us or them. If we don't have this love, we are sociopaths. If we can't identify risks, we lack foresight. So fear and anxiety are simply signs that we are normally adjusted social creatures embarking on challenging hard work. Good for us.

The bravest among us make room for fear and anxiety and keep moving forward. Actually, here's the secret. You are already making room for fear and anxiety and moving forward. The Roman philosopher Seneca taught us that "to live is an act of courage." Fear will come. Anxiety will try to weigh you down. Accept that they will be with you on the journey. You're moving ahead anyway, and while you accept that they have to come along, you are not tolerating any of their bullshit along the way.

Practice Hope

The work is scary. You will fail. Facing this, it might seem the only rational thing to do is stop before you even get started. Pull up the covers and turn out the lights and stay safe in your bed, waiting out the injustices of the world around you.

But there is one tool you can wield to beat back fear and setbacks, one tool to push you forward. Hope.

To understand how this works, it's important to agree on two things about hope. First, as Brené Brown teaches us, "hope is not an emotion." It is not like happiness or sadness, which come at us on their own. It is not a whim we try to capture and harness. Instead, "hope is a cognitive behavioral process." The psychologist CR Snyder researched hope extensively. He found that hope has two basic components: the ability to see pathways to your desired goal and the ability to motivate yourself to pursue those pathways. When we come across obstacles to meeting our goals, hope is a choice about how we will process this new information and make meaning of these challenges as we keep moving toward them.

Second, hope is learned in struggle and strengthened in adversity. When we face down obstacles that threaten to beat us back—overcoming them through our own fortitude, good thinking, and the support of our community—we strengthen our ability to hope through future challenges. Once again, Brené Brown shares that we hone our skill of hope "when we experience adversity, when we have relationships that are trustworthy, when people have faith in our ability to get out of a jam." Hope is not the ethereal fairy dust of "everything will be perfect," which makes us soft. No, hope is tough. Hope is battle-worn.

The dirty little secret here is that hope needs struggle to thrive. Struggle is the fuel that lights the fires of hope. Every obstacle we overcome, big or small, adds kindling to our hope. If we survived the last struggle—or last hundred struggles—hope whispers to us, "I bet you can survive this one too."

A few weeks before I started my first job leading a team when I was in my late twenties, I decided to host a team retreat for the ten people on staff. But I had no idea where to do it. I was moving to Los Angeles from the San Francisco Bay Area and didn't know the city, didn't have relationships. I would literally lie awake at night worried that the day of the retreat would come, and I still wouldn't have a place to host us. The uncertainty about how to find a gathering spot for ten people sent me into an anxiety tailspin. I can see now that I was so worried about being a first-time leader in a new organization in a new city that the thought of stumbling through even the smallest failures of leadership filled me with real dread.

Reading this, you can probably see how ridiculous this is. And looking back now, I can laugh at it. But that hindsight for me is hard-earned. And I don't want to downplay how difficult anxiety is. Since that time, though, I have faced more profound challenges in the work: Having one month to raise one million dollars to meet my team's budget, though I wasn't sure where it would come from. Running for public office in a high-profile race and losing. Starting a new job in a new field thousands of miles from where I built my career. And in each step, I survived and even thrived. I didn't always succeed, but I made it through the struggle and was just fine on the other side.

So now when the next challenge emerges, I simply ask myself, "What evidence do I have that this will be the problem that beats me?" I stare at the contours of the looming uncertainty and pay attention to how my mind whips up failure scenarios and my body clenches in a familiar routine. And then I remind myself that no problem, in my forty years of struggle, has left me crumpled to the ground, unable to get up for long. Most problems have evaporated or been beaten back. So I practice hope. I use what I have learned from past adversity and realize that while I don't know exactly how this obstacle will be overcome, it most certainly will be beat. "If you are on your own path, things are going to come to you," Joseph Campbell teaches us. So I put one foot in front of the other and go forward.

To practice hope well, we have to distinguish it from its dangerous twin: expectations. If hope is the process of seeing our way through the challenges ahead, expectations are the belief in a concrete treat at the end. Buddhists say that "expectations are disappointments in the making." The narrower our expectations, the more likely we are to miss the mark. If our joy is tied up with only one particular outcome—one job, one donor coming through, one champion praising our work—success becomes harder to achieve.

When expectations rise in my mind and grab ahold of my thoughts, I move deeper and ask myself what the more central hope is. I replace "I want this exact job" with "I hope I land meaningful work." I replace "I need this donor to say yes" with "I hope we have the resources we need to do our work." I replace "Please let this person praise my work" with "I hope as many people as possible get behind what we are doing." "Have hope, not expectations," a character on a TV show I watched once shared. I think that is spot on.

As the poet Reverend Victoria Safford charges us, "Our mission is to plant ourselves at the gates of Hope." Hope, she tells us, is the place where "you glimpse not only struggle, but joy in the struggle." Hope is the place where joy meets struggle. That is the path forward.

Just like the divers I watched while my daughter napped, there will be times in your life when you stand with toes curled on the edge of something exciting. You will feel the pull toward something important. Yet you will also sense the risk and crave the perceived safety of solid ground.

Success is not guaranteed, nor is it a surefire sign of your talent or worth. You might be great at the work or just good at it or maybe even awful at it. Put in the work, practice, get better at it. You may succeed or fail. But if you are called to it, do it anyway. I am not saying tilt at windmills. Don't chase every random opportunity without regard for strategy or good planning or a reasoned measure of risk. But there will always be a mountain of excuses not to leap. So if the work is where your heart's greatest desire meets the world's greatest need, do it. I can't promise you all will be rosy. But I can tell you that the world is a more beautiful, vibrant place when each of us is willing to jump into what we are uniquely called to. As Father Greg Boyle teaches us, "Look before you leap. But leap."

3

The Work Is the Work

I was exhausted, not the head-clogging tired of days with little sleep I would face later with a newborn daughter but the soul-depleting tired of years overworked. I was thirty-one years old and had been running an education nonprofit in Los Angeles for three years. We had a staff of thirty—up from nine when I started—who worked with four hundred teachers every day in some of the most overburdened schools throughout the city. Our annual budget—and the voracious fundraising drive to support it—had doubled to over five million dollars. I was drowning in the push for numbers and growth, numbers and growth.

Everything seemed to weigh on my shoulders. The lives of tens of thousands of students being taught every day by our teachers. The well-being of these teachers. The satisfaction of our staff. And the relentless fundraising. I was running Lewis Carroll's Red Queen's race—running as fast as I could just to stay in place. And it was crushing me.

So one Saturday afternoon, I wandered into a neighborhood bookstore hoping to find some inspiration. I knew whatever I needed to break through this exhaustion wasn't something I already had. I needed to find someone else to give me new tools or a new frame.

In this aimless search through book stacks, I stumbled upon the *Bhagavad Gita*, the ancient Hindu religious text. I hadn't cracked this book since college. But I remember being moved to tears reading it ten years before in the basement of the labyrinthian university library. Maybe, I thought, there would be hope in these pages.

I bought a copy and walked next door to the Belgian restaurant. I sidled up to the bar, ordered a beer and some fries, and cracked the stiff cover open. As the sunlight and breeze filtered through the opened floor-to-ceiling windows, I began to read.

I came upon a verse that drew from wisdom so deep that it would provide solace and guidance for me for years to come. In the early part of the *Gita*, a major battle in a long-standing war among family members is set to begin. The main figure, Arjuna, struggles over whether he should go into battle to fight his cousins. He frets about the impending struggle—about killing those he loves. The god Krishna tells him to basically get over himself. Stop worrying about whether he will win or lose. Just perform his duty. Krishna tells Arjuna, "You have a right to your actions, but never to your action's fruits. Act for action's sake."

Act for action's sake. Bam.

I was being shaped in a powerful work culture where the relentless pursuit of results was the first core value. A culture where strategic planning and urgency drove us forward. A culture where big wins and measurable impact were celebrated. A culture steeped in an awareness that the injustice young people of color faced in our country was so immoral that it must be wiped out as quickly as possible.

And here Krishna was saying to act, damnit, but also to let go. Do what was needed. Do not shirk from the duty. But do it because the work must be done, not because you are wedded to the outcome. Here, in this two-thousand-year-old text, I found hints of my struggles and my hopes. I saw the anxiety, the uncertainty, and the drive. And I saw a way to understand and manage this. I didn't feel so tired and afraid. In those verses, I found calm and assurance.

The work is the work. That is what the *Gita* teaches.

The work is not the outcome. The work is not the praise or the success or the win. The work is not the realization that you have done right and are talented. The work is not even making the lives of those around you better. Those are all by-products of the work. If we are lucky, that is the direction toward which the work heads. But they are not the work. Only the work is the work.

For those of us on the path to make the world around us a better place, I hope there are many victories. But we are not called to the winners' circle. We are not even called to improve and change the world around us. We are simply called to do the work. To wake up every day, drink that coffee, roll up our sleeves, and walk out that door to work the fields of our duties.

So how do we understand this seeming contradiction? How do we care deeply about sating the "world's deepest hunger" while not becoming consumed by it? How do we fight for justice with peace in our hearts?

Perhaps to help understand this tension, a story is in order. Borrowing from wise teachers over millennia, a parable might be called for.

The Parable of the Village

In a remote village in a remote country in a remote time, a terrible plague weaved its way through the people. For a while, the residents were distraught in grief and burdened by their unending care for the dying, overwhelmed by anxiety over who would be next. One day, an elderly scholar, having pored through pages of long-forgotten texts, found a possible end to the plague. Centuries prior, when a similar plague befell the village, a plant whose leaves could be boiled to distill a cure was brought back from the top of a high mountain. This mountaintop was a hard week's journey away.

Three young women were chosen for the task of harvesting the plant. Each had been spared the grips of the plague. Each was strong and bright and good. They needed to be, for this journey was beset with possible dangers. Much of the path was steep and rocky, full of opportunities to fall and be injured alone in the wilderness. The route was at most a best guess, and becoming lost was a significant risk.

On a damp and cloudy morning, the village elders gathered to send them off, each with provisions and a copy of an ancient map.

Acknowledging that the journey was long and arduous, the first young woman prayed humbly. She accepted the many dangers that could befall her and gave herself fully up to the powers of the universe to guide her. If it were destined for her to find the plant and save her village, she would. If she were not so destined, she would not. She packed up the map—for what was a man-made map when it was up to the universe to take her along the course?—and she set out at a casual pace. She went to bed early each night and woke late, for the trail was difficult, and she needed her rest to keep going. She stopped frequently along the way to admire the beauty before her eyes, and she ate often, for the journey took much energy. In a short time, her fellow travelers were multiple days ahead of her, and she fell farther and farther behind.

The second young woman was on fire with the knowledge that the villagers depended on her to reach the mountaintop and bring back the plant. She was determined to get to the top as quickly as possible and save her people. Each morning she plotted the most direct course forward. She stopped every hour to consult the map and confirm she was on the best possible route. She hiked each day well into the evening darkness and woke early each morning to get on her way, sleeping only a few hours each night. Along the path, her mind was perpetually in the future, alternating between states of anticipated joy she would experience when her village was safe and anticipated despair over what would happen if she failed. At one point, she lost nearly a half day at a fork in the road because she could not determine which direction to choose and was so afraid of making the wrong choice and failing her loved ones. Distracted in her thoughts, she eventually failed to see a rock in her path, and she stumbled, twisting her ankle. Exhausted, frazzled, and injured, she was laid out to rest for days.

The third young woman's heart was heavy. She knew the journey was hard and the work mattered greatly. If she and her fellow travelers succeeded, her village would be saved. If they failed, her loved ones would suffer and die. She was determined to do everything she could to save her village, and simultaneously she accepted that there was much outside her control along the way. Each morning, she headed out at a strong but manageable pace. At lunch each day, she stopped briefly to renourish and replot her route, and then she headed on. She stopped before nightfall to avoid traveling in the dangerous dark. At the campfire each night, she thought lovingly of her family. And in going to sleep, she put away concerns of success or failure and allowed herself a good night's rest. When she came upon the fork in the road that had proved such a conundrum for the second woman, she consulted her map for a few minutes, made the best choice she could with the information she had, and moved forward.

In this way, after a week, the third woman arrived at the mountaintop to discover an abundance of the plant she sought. She harvested a heavy bag full of the lifesaving cure. On the way back down, she came upon her fellow travelers. At each meeting, they repackaged the heavy burden of the plant equally among them, and two weeks after they'd first set off, all three entered the village together with the bags of the plant. The village was saved.

Like each of the three women, you may want to save your village. But how you orient yourself toward that outcome matters a great deal. Too little focus on it and you will fall behind. Too much focus on the outcome and you will lose your ability to progress along the journey well. The solution lies in the tricky balance the *Gita* outlines: letting the work be the work.

The parable, then, helps illuminate many of the false guides that we all follow when we avoid letting the work be the work. Their calls can be hypnotic, and their draw can be alluring. But in the end, the message of the false prophets—to spend one's time caring too little or too much about the outcomes—pulls us off course.

The False Guides of Inurgency: Self-Centering and Inaction

I know of no one who is indifferent to the outcome they work toward. I am surrounded by people fighting for a better world and a brighter future. Perhaps you are too or one day may be. Many are called to this work because the injustices they see around them are too much to bear. The first woman in the parable, if you stopped and asked her along the way, would not say she lacked urgency to remedy the plight of her village, nor was she ambivalent about its salvation. But her practice did not center deep care over her village's future at the heart of her journey. I think of her journey as one of inurgency as to the result. It is not the big-picture indifference to the outcome, for she was as determined as the others; it was that she brought an everyday practice of indifference to justice's call for quick realization.

The masthead of this inurgency is borne by two false beliefs about how justice is served. The first false belief is the commitment to self-centering. By this, I mean placing one's personal needs and wants as the primary focus of the work. I don't want to confuse self-centering, which is the focus on oneself, with self-care, which is the necessary nurturing of oneself so one can do the work. Self-care is different for each of us. It is rest, time with loved ones, taking care of one's body, pursuing hobbies, or intentionally participating in any set of activities which strengthens us and grounds us. Self-care is critical. My sister uses a helpful airplane safety analogy for this. When life brings me to a frazzle point, she reminds me I have to put the oxygen mask on myself before I can put it on others. I recently heard someone tell me, "You can't pour from an empty cup," reminding me that if I seek to give of myself to the world—my love, grace, patience, empathy, hard work— my physical and emotional cup should be full enough to offer it out. We can't give what we don't have.

Whatever analogy we use, grounding ourselves in the importance of self-care in the work is essential. But self-care is not self-centering. While self-care allows us to take on new challenges, self-centering protects us from exerting ourselves too much or taking on too big of a risk. While self-care gives us the strength to challenge our friends and colleagues on behalf of the communities we serve, self-centering gives us a way out from engaging in conflict with our allies. While self-care allows us to deflect unproductive feedback or perceived slights in order to move forward, self-centering encourages us to wallow in indignation and gossip about those who hurt us. Taking care of oneself so that we can engage in the work is essential. Centering our wants and comforts in our work's focus is obstructionist.

The second false belief that inurgency manifests is a commitment to either inaction or unnecessarily slow action. While pace should not be our focus, pace matters. The injustices we confront should not exist one day longer than they absolutely have to. Moving with indifference or slowness of pace related to that urgency is tolerance of that injustice.

The sidelines of the US civil rights movement are littered with well-intentioned white people lulled to inaction. Locked in a jail in Birmingham, Alabama, Dr. Martin Luther King Jr. railed against the "white moderate . . . who paternalistically believes he can set the timetable for another man's freedom; who lives by a mythical concept of time and who constantly advises the Negro to wait for a 'more convenient season.'" Nina Simone sings to us in "Mississippi Goddam" about the pain of being told to pump the brakes on the march toward full equality. "Me and my people just about due," she sings. "I've been there, so I know. They say, 'Go slow!' But that's just the trouble."

Looking back on history, the calls from white politicians to slow down the movement toward justice can seem confounding, foolish. And, yes, the blame that your generation will lay at my generation's feet for not doing enough or fast enough is fair. But how many times will you sit in meetings just to be told you'll revisit the question in a few months' time? How many times will leaders tell you, as a younger person, to wait your turn before you can assume leadership to right some community wrong? How many times has my generation kicked the can down the road never to have followed up or followed through? For those with privilege brought by skin color, money, or gender, the siren song of inurgency assails us with numbness no matter how deeply we care about the issue or the people being harmed.

A few years back, I joined a small group of civil rights leaders who had been meeting twice a year, ruminating on how to reform a particular law that was unjustly placing people at risk of prosecution. Outside this group, I had spoken with a number of individuals who were at risk from the effects of this law, and they were adamant that it should be changed immediately. At my third meeting with this group of civil rights leaders, tired of inaction, I tried to push the group to set a timeline and a series of next steps that would move us more quickly toward reform. The participants balked at the push and insisted more had to be done before a timeline could be set. And just as I saw before, once again, the group adjourned with a commitment to revisit the issue in a few weeks' time.

After that meeting, one of the key leaders called me to challenge my thinking and approach. He told me the group had been meeting for *six years* on the matter and that the conversations had been "productive" and "successful." When I asked what movement had been made, he conceded "none yet," but he promised to reconvene the group shortly to move the ball forward. The next meeting took place four months later with no actions taken in the interim.

In similar ways, white moderates in Martin Luther King Jr.'s time or the civil rights leader asking me to slow down for more conversation mirrored the first woman in the Parable of the Village. Yes, they may have truly cared about righting the wrongs people experienced. But their wants were not strong enough to force them to change, to spur them faster toward full liberation at the pace justice required.

The False Guides of Outcome Obsession: Paralysis and Freneticism

While inurgency to justice's speedy realization holds us back from engaging meaningfully in the work, so does a hyper-urgent obsession with whether our work will lead to justice. We are called to the work of justice because our world is steeped in pain. We see and hear and feel deep trauma and rabid inequities. And this witness is so often personal. For the pain of the world is often carried by those least emboldened to do so—the young and the old, the weak and the sick, the inheritors of intergenerational mistreatment.

Many of us in the work share identity or even community with those carrying the largest weight of these burdens. But like the second woman on the journey to the mountaintop, we can become so caught up in obsession and anxiety about getting to that future state that we don't realize we are inhibited from doing the best work to get there. Outcome obsession is heralded most forcefully by two false ideas.

The first false guide is paralysis. In facing the daunting task of chipping away at the mountain of injustice, we may suffer from analysis paralysis. When faced with a tough decision or uncertainty about how to move forward, you may ask yourself over and over again, "What if I talked to one more person about this difficult decision? What if I read one more writer on the matter? What if I reviewed one more study on the issue?"

Often paralysis shows up, simply, as spinning the wheels. We hold the implicit belief that if we keep mulling it over, we can control how it unfolds. As you have learned by now, I am predisposed to anxiety. I fret. I obsess. I mull. A good planner plans and then executes. But a spinner plans and then replans and replans. And I can spin.

In my early years leading nonprofits, I would constantly worry about raising enough money to meet our budget. In the office, I would map out the best plan I could. Then I would ruminate over it on the drive home. I would play out scenarios in the shower. I would lie awake at night revisiting the plan. In short, I wore a rut in the cognitive path in my mind around the uncertainty I was trying to control. But spinning isn't the work. It's a distraction from the work and a waste of energy. Like a cyclist on a grounded bike, it's all movement and no progress.

The second of these false guides is the opposite of paralysis—freneticism. The moving around at high speeds, flitting from one action to another, constantly worrying whether one is on the right path, and frequently changing direction. We are often just doing something because it feels like we're doing something.

In 2012, I was a candidate for the California State House of Representatives. Early in the campaign, I met with one of the top campaign experts in the state, hoping to hire him. He never ended up working for me, but he gave me some of the best advice about campaigns and about the work in general. He said that in any campaign, there is more work to be done—more voters to convince, more donors to meet, more volunteers to inspire—than can possibly be done. And in the midst of a campaign, there are a million things that you can do to give your campaign some small boost. But you can't be distracted by that. Determine a plan, a plan that is smart enough and good enough, and stick to that. If you don't, you'll be pulled in a million directions and never move forward. This wasn't an advice to stick blindly to a bad plan; it was advice to have a plan and change it rarely and only when it makes absolute sense. But in the meantime, work your plan and don't fret about all the other things that could be done. The rest is just noise.

The *Gita* may tell us that we do not have a right to the fruit of our actions, but Gandhi added that "renunciation of fruit in no way means indifference to the result." In fact, caring about the result is critical. We have to know what is an expected result of an action so that we can decide if it is the right next step. We have to think critically and work hard to make sure we are on the right path toward greater justice.

But what renunciation in this context means is the "absence of hankering after fruit." Gandhi teaches, "He who is ever brooding over result often loses nerve in the performance of his duty. He becomes impatient and then gives vent to anger and begins to do unworthy things; he jumps from action to action never remaining faithful to any. He who broods over results . . . is ever distracted."

At the end of the day, outcome obsession—whether via paralysis or freneticism—is just a waste of energy. The work takes a lot from us. It requires generosity even in the face of selfishness. It requires calm in the face of panic. It requires vigilance—waking up every day and turning to the work even when things are difficult. We must pour from ourselves the emotional energy the work requires, remembering that one of the worst things we can do is spill from the cup. The energy we have to do this work is finite. It can be added to, for sure, but it always has a limit.

The waste of emotional energy in this work is cruel, what Annie Dillard defines as the waste of pain. When we put ourselves through the emotional ringer by fretting about the outcomes and perseverating over all that might come our way, we pour out our emotional energy onto the concrete. We waste our pain. It does not better others or enhance our ability to do the work. It is cruel to ourselves, who deserve to deploy what we have in ways that make the world around us better. And it is cruel to others, who are denied our best selves and our best work.

An Elephant Balancing on a Ball

This is what the *Gita* and the Parable of the Village teach us. We are called to do the work with active determination and without obsession over the outcome. This calling is both liberating and challenging.

It is liberating because it reminds us that we can let go of the outcomes of our work. We can have the clearest vision and the most strategic plan and be the most talented and work the hardest, but those things only narrow the gap between our actions and the impact we want to see. At the end of the day, like the handsome TV writer said on our third date, the rest has to be covered by grace. The rest always has to be covered by grace.

It is challenging because it reminds us that we will never arrive. Like in the Hebrew Bible where Moses struggled to lead his people out of Egypt and ended up wandering the desert for forty years but was never permitted to enter the Promised Land, we are only called to set out on the journey. We are not promised the win. We are not promised the chance to see the benefits of the work. We are simply called to set out on the road and walk it daily. That is the work.

This is where the words of Miley Cyrus come in handy. Stay with me on this one. Her song "The Climb" captures what the *Gita* tries to teach us:

> *There's always gonna be another mountain. I'm*
> *always gonna wanna make it move.*
> *Always gonna be an uphill battle. Sometimes I'm*
> *gonna have to lose.*
> *Ain't about how fast I get there. Ain't about what's*
> *waiting on the other side.*
> *It's the climb.*

That's it. It's not about getting to the top. There is no top. There may be points of respite—of reflection or satisfaction—but the point of the work is not about finishing it. It's about the climb.

But the climb is a lot. The climb is putting one foot in front of the other, often on a rocky path and a steep pitch. We climb when we are tired. We climb even when we are scared. We climb when we feel we lack the tools and worry it will all be for naught. When the *Gita* says, "You have a right to your actions," it is set in a section about the moral duty to act.

This is the fundamental mind screw of the *Gita*'s proscription. We can neither be indifferent to the outcomes nor taken over by obsession with outcomes. Like a circus elephant standing on a ball, this delicate balance is not easy to pull off. We are always falling off and having to slowly and often unsteadily climb back on.

The only way I know how to pull this off—and what I think the *Gita* is getting at—is to stay focused on the work itself. University of Alabama football coach Nick Saban has some insight here. As of writing this, Alabama has won nearly 90 percent of all games and has claimed six national championships under his leadership. When he coaches his players, he insists they stay out of the future. "Don't think about the national championship," he admonishes. "Think about what you needed to do in this drill, on this play, in this moment. That's the process: Let's think about what we can do today, the task at hand." At its core, he reminds his players to "trust the process"—that if you get and stay good at the nitty-gritty of the work, victories will unfold. But if you focus on the victories, you are too distracted to get good at the work.

Care about the outcomes. Plan to get there as quickly as possible. Pay attention to where you may be off course so you can redirect. But don't lose yourself in fretting about the outcomes. Just do the work for the work's sake.

In the end, you are not fully in control over whether you arrive. But brooding over whether or not you will get there won't help get you there. Neither will waiting passively for change. Just climb. And when your lumbering pachyderm of a mind falls off that ball—when you find yourself focused too much on the outcomes or doing too little to advance the work—gently get your wobbly legs right back on the ball.

And So We Fly

Everyone I respect—great and small, famous and unknown, celebrated and ignored—is in the end forgotten. That may not be a comforting thought, but to me it reminds me that it's the work that remains. I have a small piece of paper taped above my desk at home right now, and on it I have written myself a reminder: "Everyone is forgotten on a long enough time horizon." So don't worry about what may be. Just do the work.

Henri Nouwen, the great spiritual writer, tells the story about his brief time traveling with a group of trapeze artists. I knew he would be a great thinker and spiritual mentor when I learned he was willing to take up with a circus troupe. Nouwen befriended a trapeze artist named Rodleigh, whose dazzling performance was the centerpiece of the show. "How does it work?" Nouwen asked. "The secret," Rodleigh shared, "is that the flyer does nothing and the catcher does everything. When I fly to Joe, I simply have to stretch out my arms and hands and wait for him to catch me." He continued, "The worst thing the flyer can do is to try to catch the catcher. . . . If I grabbed Joe's wrists, I might break them, or he might break mine. . . . A flyer must fly and . . . [he] must trust, with outstretched arms, that his catcher will be there for him."

Maybe this is how we are supposed to let the work be the work. Maybe we should just accept ourselves as who we are: dazzling, bejeweled, vibrant flying-trapeze artists. Yes, we must practice every day. Yes, we must seek out true companions who will catch us. We must string up a safety net. We must start small and grow bigger through calculated risks. We must fall and learn and do again. But when it comes to it, we must let go of the trapeze and fly through the air, trusting in the arc and the catcher. If we fail to work hard at the work, we will lack the precision and the skill to land the flight. But if we obsess about it, we may seize up in midair or grab frantically at the catcher and break their wrists. So we do the work—and we fly.

Plan for a perfect routine. Practice with particular outcomes in mind. And when you get out there, care deeply about being successful. But when you let go and fly with arms outstretched, do so fully ready to accept the outcome ahead of you.

4

Seek First to Understand

It was the type of hot September evening I loved, the only time of the year Los Angeles nights warmed like the southern nights of my childhood. Forty families crowded into a single sixth-grade classroom. Parents occupied every conceivable space. Middle-aged men and women crouched into middle school chairs, adult legs trapped under middle school desks. They sat on the teacher's desk. They leaned against corners of the room. They were anxious. I was anxious. But about different things.

I had started in my role as head of schools three weeks earlier. This was a critical juncture for our community.

The school district only authorized our school to run to sixth grade. We now could petition the district to allow us to extend to eighth grade or beyond. Or we could accept with finality that sixth grade would be as far as our school went. If the former—and if the district granted our request—parents were guaranteed a seventh-grade placement for their child. If the latter, they had to scramble right now to find a school for their child for the following year.

Our timeline was tight. To get a decision from the district in time for us to open a seventh grade, our petition was due in less than a month. And believe me when I say few people are more intense than nervous parents. This gathering was high stakes for a new head of schools.

But I was prepared. I had spent my first few weeks on the job talking to board members, working with the principal, and conducting a strategic analysis. In that hot and crowded classroom, I announced with confidence that we would open a middle school. Not even a month into the job, barely known to the parents in front of me, I laid out a vision for the middle school. It would mirror our elementary school. It would be diverse. It would center the child in the learning process. It would be academically rigorous.

It was this last word that triggered the room. I missed it at first, so unfamiliar with this community, so caught up in my performance. Then I called on Chris, who had raised her hand defiantly. "Who are you," she began, "to unilaterally change the mission of this entire school?"

Stunned, I listened as she continued to challenge me. "What makes the school so special is its nurturing environment. Now you propose to change it into a high-pressure academic mill?"

Parents murmured and nodded as she spoke. They eyed me expectantly.

I tried to recover. I told her I had no intention of changing the heart and soul of the school. By *rigorous*, I meant a commitment to making sure each child reached their fullest potential. The room seemed to accept this explanation, at least skeptically.

As the parents poured out and I closed the evening with short conversations here and there, it hit me. I really didn't know what these parents wanted for their children. I knew what the board wanted. I knew what the principal wanted. I knew what I was inspired by. But I didn't really understand what these parents wanted.

So I began to listen. Not simply to hear or engage but to understand. I met parents where they were—in classrooms after school, at coffee shops in the neighborhood, in living rooms. I met parents one-on-one. I met parents in small gatherings in their homes, where we sat stuffed onto small couches in cramped living rooms.

At each of these meetings, I started by asking parents what they wanted. What type of school environment would make them want to keep their child here for seventh grade? What were they afraid of for their child? What were they excited about? Who did they want their child to be? How did they want a school to help their child grow into this person?

As the answers came, I slowly began to weave a picture of a school community these parents wanted. A place that supported their children to do well, not pushed them. A place that inspired their children to learn, not pressured them. A place that understood their child's unique strengths and talents and quirks and met them where they were.

While I understood that their desires were aligned and wholly complementary to the academic rigor I heard from the school staff, by beginning to understand what families wanted, I could meaningfully address the entire school community and work in solidarity to create a vision aligned to the hopes and goals of many.

In reflecting on that first meeting in September, I realize I was so focused on doing good *to* the community that I failed to focus on doing good *with* and *for* the community. It's not that my initial plan was wrong. Rightness and wrongness were distracting questions. It's that my initial plan was incomplete. It lacked the deep understanding of the community I was brought in to serve.

The only way to develop that understanding was to reach out, head into the community, and listen, listen, listen. It wasn't to plan or analyze or strategize. It was first to seek to understand.

There's a story from the Hebrew Bible I think of often, especially as I am drawn to the prophets and how the prophetic tradition has informed many justice movements.

In this story, the prophet Elijah is on the run. Queen Jezebel is hunting him down after he bested her prophets in a large public ceremony. I have a picture of Elijah racing, stumbling forward, wide-eyed into the night, until he collapses in the town of Beersheba. An angel visits him and tells him to go to Mount Sinai and wait until he hears the voice of God.

Elijah does what he is told. Huddles in a cave carved into the mountainside. Waits.

Soon, a deafening and powerful wind whips across the slope. But the voice of God is not in the wind.

Soon, the mountain shakes with the force of a rageful earthquake. But the voice of God is not in the earthquake.

Soon, a fire tears up the face of the mountain. With a roaring crackle, it devours everything in its path. But the voice of God is not in the fire.

Then everything dies down. And things get quiet. In the wake of noise and furor, a very small sound comes, a gentle whisper. A voice. The voice of God is in that soft-ness. Elijah pulls his cloak over his face to show respect in the presence of that awesomeness. And he goes out to greet the voice.

What I discovered reading that text is that truth and insight are rarely found in the cacophony. Our world is overwhelmed with so many strong and competing voices. We are pontificated to on cable news channels. We are raged at over social media. We are revved up at rallies. There has never been a time when so many voices reach up and out with such force. We live in a time of wind and earthquakes and fire.

What we need to hear is rarely found in the loud-est voices. Truth is found in the in-between spaces. The spaces most of us fail to pay attention to. It is found in the quieter voices. The voices left on the mountainside after the storms have raged on.

For each of us, these voices are found in different places. When I worked with the schools, I discovered them in the students, the teachers, and the parents—and often the parents who rarely showed up at school meetings, the ones I had to seek out. Today, I find those gathered voices in coffee shops and church basements and library meet-ing rooms in communities. The places leaders, politicians, and self-proclaimed changemakers often forget to go or rarely seek out. For you one day, maybe it will be found in the voices of your children. In your colleagues who show up and do the work but hardly ever speak in meetings. In your patients who rarely come or miss appointments and even more rarely ask questions. In your clients whose voices seem most lost.

That story of the prophet Elijah reminds me these voices must be sought out. He did not wait in the relative comfort and hiddenness of Beersheba, surrounded by ample food and protective friends, for the voice of God to find him. He sought out that voice. He searched for the place where he believed the voice lived. And when he got to the mountainside, he waited for that voice. He pushed through the noise and the fear until he found the voice. And finally, when he found it, he walked out humbly to greet it.

It's those quiet voices in our lives we're called to seek out too.

It is not enough to wait expectantly in your living room or office, ready for the voices to knock on your door. The work calls to you to meet the voices where they are. To pick up the phone. To send the email. To show up in the community. To knock on the colleague's door. To bend the ear away from the noise to the very quiet voice.

The work calls us to ask. To seek to be invited in. To risk the humiliation of being rebuffed. To accept silence. To reveal our ignorance. To begin with our humility.

The one voice Elijah needed to hear above all others was so quiet it had to be sought out. The voices the work calls us to are quiet as well—and they are only heard when we seek them out and wait and listen.

Yes, the noise will rage around you, but to pull forth these voices from the noise, there are dual talismans for your understanding: curiosity and love.

Curiosity is the head. Curiosity is the recognition that others hold a piece of the answer. It is the hunger for that wisdom. The drive to know what they know. It is the reaching out to others—past our own borders—to learn what part of the solution these others hold.

Love is the heart. Love is the acknowledgment of our incompleteness paired with the yearning for completeness. It is looking across the chasm of our separateness to others—with and for whom we work—and beholding their essentialness. It is the soulful recognition that we are bound to others in this work.

Curiosity is the drive to seek the wisdom in others. Love is the belief that holders of this wisdom matter.

When your priority is first to understand, you'll not only discover better and more complete answers, but the listening will also fuel the trust and connection helping you do the work well. People can tell when we don't care all that much about them but have an agenda *for* them, even if it's a good and well-meaning agenda. You will come to know people who, as the adage says, love humanity but hate people. Nobody wants to be helped by someone who likes them in the abstract but can't stand them in solid form right in front of their eyes. Communities who have been scourged by decades of trauma are listeners for the true voice too. They will wait out the inevitable waves of lukewarm helpers and talkers who come and go. Until the listener partners show up.

Doing the work requires you to be honest with yourself. What exactly are you playing at if you aren't curious about and don't love the people you are working for?

To put your time and strength and talents into people who you just aren't that interested in is not the work. If that is the case, you're better off doing something else. Woodworking. Investment banking. Marathon running. Anything else.

But keep showing up with curiosity and love, and the tendrils of connection begin to form. Sometimes this takes days. Sometimes years.

Spend enough time showing up. Keep respectfully asking questions and honoring the answers. Over time, walls that may have seemed insurmountable begin to crack a little. It is through these cracks, as Leonard Cohen teaches us, that the light gets in. Not every wall will crack.

You will not connect with every person. Walls are there for a reason. They don't break open just because we want them to. But some will. And when the walls crack, people are more willing to share with us what we need to know to partner with them better. Trust, which stems from these connections, helps the work move forward—and faster.

Not only do curiosity and love fuel the way we meet our communities, but they are also the fuel that keeps us going. Mikara Solomon Davis, one of the most inspiring principals I ever met, led Ralph Bunche Elementary in Compton for six years. During this time, she transformed one of the lowest-performing schools in California into one of the highest-performing ones. I don't say this lightly: she is magical.

When asked what she looked for in hiring new teachers, she simply said, "First and foremost, you have to love kids. I can teach you the craft of being a good teacher, but I can't teach you to love kids." Admittedly, loving kids isn't enough on its own. But you can't do much as a teacher for long if you don't have that groundwork. Loving the kids—and being curious enough about what makes each child tick—is the reason you can stand getting out of bed before dawn five days a week. Loving kids is what keeps you grading and lesson planning at eight o'clock at night. Loving kids is what makes you laugh at the craziness unfolding in your classroom instead of pulling your hair out and screaming until you are hoarse. OK, sometimes that even happens when you love kids. As a former first-grade teacher, as a father, I can tell you that loving kids isn't all hugs and mush and euphoria. But it is often the well of energy that keeps you going when caffeine and sleep and emotional fortitude have all left you.

That's what makes a drive to seek first to understand so powerful. Sure, it gets us to better answers. But it also connects us to our communities and gives us more staying power in the work for the long haul.

Seeking first to understand isn't only about getting to good answers in close partnership with others. It is also a great tool to take on the opposition.

Everyone is the hero of their own story. Everyone takes their life experiences, the worldviews of their loved ones, and the opinions of those whom they respect and builds a narrative that makes sense of the world around them. We then behave in accordance with that worldview. Sometimes we do this purposefully. Often we do not.

In decades of doing the work, I am hard-pressed to think of anyone I met who woke up every day thinking, "Today I am going to screw over good people."

In my current work leading the LGBTQ+ civil rights organization in my home state, I often come up against opposition. Sometimes this opposition comes from our peers and partners. More often it is opposition from those on the other side of the aisle. If we need to change the opposition's mind or move against them, we can ask one simple question first: why?

In their story where our opponents' actions are good, why is their opposition to us right and just? What do they believe about themselves, the world around them, and us that makes them the good guys of the story?

Answering this simple question of "why" requires so much listening. It requires the humility to cast the opponents as heroes and to cast ourselves, as they may see us, as villains. It requires creativity and openness to a new way of thinking. To do it well, it requires some level of relationship with our opponents. It requires curiosity and love.

This is not to say we legitimize all of our opponents' actions or beliefs. Understanding the motives that fuel them does not require us to give them a free pass. We can understand the "why" behind actions and still conclude those actions are unjust. But when we understand their story, we can determine how best to move the opponent, move around the opponent, or beat the opponent.

A few years ago, a parent of a transgender child met with me in a hip Chicago coffee shop that used to be a bike repair store. Over midafternoon coffees, she shared how anxious her daughter was about going to the restroom in public. She was always afraid she would be called out by some fellow patron, well-meaning or otherwise, and told to go to the men's room. This was particularly maddening, the mother told me, when restrooms were single-stall only. One toilet, one locked door. Why did it matter if it were a men's room or a women's room? Couldn't all single-stall bathrooms be gender-neutral, open to everyone?

I agreed. My team and I began to dive in. We researched the underlying laws. We talked to potentially allied groups. We sat down with labor and management: the plumbers and the restaurant and hotel associations.

Finally, we turned our attention to the opposition. We knew there was growing alarm in conservative, and even some moderate, communities about the rise of affirming laws accounting for transgender people. Some of the concerns were around safety. These concerns, while deeply felt, did not have a wide factual basis. No wave of violence had erupted in communities that had adopted more accommodating public spaces for trans people. But concerns often rose simply from anxiety about the unknown. Gender, many of us had been taught, was immutable. We were told gender corresponded, without deviation, to the bodies we were born in. If that were not true, what would happen to all the public distinctions we made about gender? What would that mean for the public distinctions in places where we felt the most vulnerable—bathrooms, locker rooms, and the like?

In planning how to engage this opposition, we first honored this anxiety. It did not mean we justified it or found the conclusions that flowed from it legitimate. It simply meant we treated this anxiety as a real factor that many people might wrestle with.

For our allied legislators, we spoke in a language we knew would get them on board. We talked about rights. We talked about historically marginalized communities feeling safe in public. We talked about justice. But for our more moderate and more conservative legislators, we talked in a language they spoke—anxiety. And we spoke to address and minimize their anxiety. We referred to the legislation as our "planes-and-trains bill." Every bathroom they had used on a plane or a train, we reminded them, had been single-occupancy and gender-neutral. Nailing that bathroom to the ground didn't make it any more dangerous. In one public hearing at the Capitol, one conservative legislator asked whether all the bill did was require a small signage change. Our chief sponsor in the House of Representative answered simply, "Yes." In order to secure the support of these legislators, we needed to convince them that a law that would be profoundly impactful for some had no real impact on most of us. There was no spin. We didn't lie. We didn't misrepresent. But to stem the potential tide of anxiety that could have overwhelmed our cause, we needed the transformative to be recognizable, familiar, banal. Suddenly, like a whisper after the noise, the anxiety was quietly and directly addressed.

The bill passed without a single no vote in either the House or the Senate. To my knowledge, this is the only transgender-affirming "bathroom bill" to pass without opposition in any state legislature in the country. This happened because we first took time to understand—and even honor—what was playing on the hearts and in the minds of conservative and moderate legislators. From a listening stance, we developed a strategy both true to the situation and to us and spoke from a common language, with understanding. This is why throughout Illinois, whenever you are in a public space and come upon a single-occupancy restroom, you see it is open to people of all genders.

Seeking first to understand is a powerful tool to minimize the opposition as well as to broaden one's base of support.

So why do we so often come across new information, new communities, new people and see them through the lens of our own predetermined conclusions? Why do we so often meet newness with answers rather than questions?

Sometimes it is a lack of imagination. Sometimes it is dogma. Sometimes it is the blinding conviction in our own rightness. Sometimes it is the fear of what may be true if we admit we do not have the answers.

When we are young, they have a word for the dam that holds back the waters of curiosity and love—*hubris*. When we get older, they call it *expertise*. Neither creates true change.

For a while, I worked with a national team of local community organizers focused exclusively on partnering with teachers and former teachers. Our first few local teams had had some initial successes. An influential leader in Colorado heard about our work and invited me to meet with a roundtable of philanthropists and statewide leaders to explore bringing our work to Colorado.

In a glass-walled conference room in downtown Denver, I sat around four tables conjoined in a square. Around these tables sat a dozen professionally dressed men and women, each with a warm smile and a reserved, discerning demeanor. It became clear this was less of a mutual exploration and more of a pitch meeting. I was expected to "sell" our work. They would then decide if they wanted to "buy" our work. So I pitched.

I began by explaining that at the heart of our work was training our teachers to go out and listen to community. This listening was meant to uncover which problems evoked deep concern in a broad swath of people. Only when a community's most critical concerns were identified did we have the fuel needed to build a coalition of concerned community members to solve the problem.

This approach was not unique to us. We borrowed freely and explicitly from Saul Alinsky, Cesar Chavez, Martin Luther King Jr., and others. But I could tell, as I was explaining this approach in our contemporary context, that I was losing the room.

Then I offered an example. Our teachers in Los Angeles believed from their own experience that school safety was an issue that was important to teachers and parents alike. They went around, in one-on-one conversations and small gatherings called *house meetings*, to ask parents and teachers about their concerns with school safety. Bullying in schools and safe passage to schools were commonly raised. But every once in a while, a teacher would say, "Did you hear about so-and-so, who was almost hit by a car on their way to school?" Or a parent would say, "I'm worried about my child crossing the busy street to get to school." Or finally, in one school community, our members heard the tragic story of a mom who had been killed by a truck on the morning walk to school when she jumped into the street to push her child out of the way.

Our teachers gathered and compared the stories they heard. They realized that the concern of safely crossing streets on the way to and from school kept coming up. Our teachers became curious. Why were so many parents and fellow teachers bringing this up? Had this always been a problem?

They asked city experts for documentation and uncovered that a few years back, during the 2008 recession, the city had cut the crossing guard budget. In the biggest car-traffic city in our country, there were almost no crossing guards guiding young children safely across busy roads to school. Our teachers were onto something, thanks to listening to parents in the community.

They began organizing people. They gathered an ever-growing network of parents and teachers to educate them on the crossing guard issue. They met with city officials and city council members. They partnered with labor groups. After a few months, with a broad base of support, they successfully pressured the Los Angeles City Council to include one million dollars a year into the city budget for crossing guards. After months of building action, tens of thousands of Los Angeles children now had a safer walk to school. This was all possible because it began with listening.

As I finished this story, a woman who had been a senior elected official and now was an influential philanthropist responded, "If we invest to bring you to Colorado and all you do is get more crossing guards, we will consider it a waste of our money."

I responded, "Then I think you may be right. We might not be a good fit for you."

This woman and her colleagues around the table thought they already knew the most important things that needed to be done to improve public education in Colorado. Maybe it was school funding. Or teacher evaluation. Or training and supporting principals better. Whatever they thought was needed, maybe they were mostly right. These were, after all, some of the smartest people working on the problem of public education in the state. They were undoubtedly experts.

But I think the question of rightness clouded their judgment. As I wrote before, the question of whether a course of action is right or wrong often conceals the more important question of whether a proposed solution is complete.

Their expertise served as a dam holding back the waters of curiosity and love.

To hear, even secondhand, the stories of parents deeply worried about whether their children could get to school each morning without being hit by a car and conclude that the work of getting more crossing guards would be a waste of money—that was the height of hubris. It ignored that parents held a major part of the solution for what made schools better for their children. And it failed to believe that these parents mattered.

When we begin with a poverty of curiosity and love, when we prefer to claim our expertise—and our rightness—we meet the single greatest block to our ability to reach out and learn from those most impacted by the work.

To suss out what they believe.

To understand what they fear.

To learn what they want.

It's important to keep in mind that working with curiosity and love does not mean abandoning ourselves in the process. We are all born with our talents and our strengths. Over time you have honed your areas of expertise. You are already undoubtedly seeing the world through the lens of your hard-earned perspective. In order to be honest in the work—to appreciate the uniqueness of who you are and what you bring—you must be willing to share your talents, your expertise, and your perspective. Or as I say to new community organizers, you don't honor people by leaving yourself at the door. But listening first allows you to know what to bring forth in order to best partner with others for change.

I once sat down with the community outreach team of a national nonprofit that had been working for over a year in a particular Chicago neighborhood. They had met one-on-one with community leaders. They had shown up at community events. They had led with humility in all their interactions. But a year into the work, they were still not being invited to tables where issues impacting the neighborhood were being discussed. They were flummoxed.

So I asked the team, "What do you bring to the table?" The question genuinely stumped them. Eyes darted to each other and then rested on the team leader. "I'm not sure," she confessed. I told them, "If you don't know what value you bring, no one is going to figure it out for you."

Leading with curiosity and love—seeking first to understand—is not about denying your skills and insights in the process. It is a false humility that ignores the valuable assets you can bring to the work. Seeking first to understand is just that. Seeking *first* to understand. Not seeking *only* to understand. Most of us are not academics sitting on the sidelines, merely charged with describing the work. And even academics are not asked to be irrelevant. We are called to inform and change the world around us.

Seeking first to understand is about starting with openness, not with conclusions.

Seeking first to understand doesn't mean rejecting your hard-won beliefs or throwing out what has made you successful.

Seeking first to understand is about leaving room for the possibility that people you do the work with and for have something essential to add. It is about wrestling with whether an answer is both right and complete.

On a late June afternoon, I stood in front of two hundred prospective teachers. They were about to start their training the next morning on a path to serving as educators in low-income communities in a half dozen cities on the West Coast. The sun was setting slowly over the Pacific as we gathered on a campus lawn perched on a bluff overlooking the ocean. The vibe was hopeful and anticipatory and a little bit anxious.

I told them about the writer Marius von Senden, who wrote that as modern surgeons began to improve their ability to remove cataracts in the late nineteenth century, they would travel across Europe and the United States performing operations curing people of blindness. Every once in a while, they came across someone who had been blind with cataracts since birth. They were able to give them the gift of sight for the first time.

Can you imagine what that must have been like? To live your entire life not knowing what colors look like. Or shapes. Or the faces of people who love you. And then all of sudden, in one moment, have your entire world changed.

Among those who had the surgery, there was one camp who totally rejected this new world. One story records a young girl so confused by the unfamiliar new sight that she refused to move around her house unless she closed her eyes. She reentered the world she was comfortable in.

But there was another group who approached this fundamental new reality with a sense of wonder and amazement. There was one girl who, on going to the garden for the first time since she gained sight, stopped in front of something. "She is greatly astonished and can scarcely be persuaded to answer," von Senden wrote. "She stands speechless in front of a tree which she only knows is a tree when she takes hold of it. And then looking at it as the tree with lights in it."

I shared with the prospective teachers that they reminded me of these newly sighted patients. Each of you, I told them, would be going into an experience in which your world would be fundamentally changed.

And like the newly sighted patients, you will constantly face a choice. You could do what some patients did and reject this new world, this new sight. You could slide back into the areas you feel comfortable in when, say, a student says something that frustrates or challenges you. Or when a fellow teacher with a different set of experiences says something that deeply offends you. Or when the principal tells you something can't be done because of this school rule or that district policy. You could wholly and utterly reject it. Retreat back into what you know and stay there.

Or you could accept the sight. You could embrace the new world around you with wonder and amazement. You could ask questions and try to make sense of what is in front of you. You could set aside judgment and conclusions, perhaps just for a moment, and seek first to understand.

And maybe, I said to them, you will learn how to be better in that moment. To appreciate something important in the newness. That the student wasn't being defiant. She was just hungry because she hadn't had a meal that day. That the teacher wasn't being a bigot. She was just issuing some tough love because her expectations of her students remained defiantly high. That the school rule or district policy wasn't bureaucratic nonsense. It actually made a quirky kind of sense.

And then again, maybe you'll find out you were right in the first place. The student was wrong. The fellow teacher was a jerk. The school rule or district policy was ridiculous.

But holding the newness in front of you with a sense of appreciation and humility first will make you better teachers, better people. It will deepen your understanding of the community around you. And over time, it will draw you closer to the people as you work with them.

So that is the charge I gave those prospective teachers. That is the charge I give myself. That is the charge I give you.

Seek first to understand. You may be right. You may be wrong. But holding back judgment and moving forward first with curiosity and love will only make your work better.

Remember how the prophet Elijah was summoned to the mountaintop to listen? It's that holy duty we're given as well—to go out, to seek out, and to listen.

When we listen with a curious mind and a loving heart, like Elijah, we move out into the world fortified with the knowledge we have gained.

Here's where the Elijah story moves next. After Elijah hears the voice of God, he knows what to do and gets right to work. He recruits someone to help him, Elisha, and sets out on the path to bring about change. So, like Elijah, we seek out the voices that are hard to hear. We listen humbly to those voices. Then we take that wisdom from others, combined with what is best in us, and move forward. We go do the work.

5

Know Why You Speak

We all want to be heard. In fact, we expect to be heard. Our wants are reasonable. Our needs are clear. So when we give voice to them, we expect all those with good sense and decent hearts to respond positively. When this doesn't happen, as is often the case, we diagnose the problem the only way that makes sense to us—the other people are incompetent or selfish or cruel.

The same is the case in the work. Many people drawn to making the world better have experienced a lifetime of injustice, personally and up close. I know, for me, I often see a better way so clearly that I could almost reach out and touch it. But when I actually try to tell others about it, I can be met with indifference or downright opposition. The conclusion I am tempted to draw—the only one that makes sense in the moment—is that those around me aren't down for the cause. They are compliant sheep willing just to go along with the hegemony. Or they are the enemies I have to rail against. While maybe that is the case—there are certainly many people who are willing to accept unjust systems and a few more willing to perpetuate them—sometimes, I've learned, I am simply being misunderstood.

Now every time I open my mouth to make the community—our world—a better place, I start by asking, "Why am I speaking?" *Am I speaking to voice my truth, or am I speaking to be heard?* We have been taught, through epic movies and dramatic stories, that by speaking our truth in the language most authentic to us, the world will open up its ears and hearts and hear what we have to say. But as my fellow activists can attest, this is rarely the case. Speaking to voice our truth centers our lives—our experiences, our language. It does not take into account the listeners' lives. It does not consider what they need to hear to understand us. When our truth and the world's ability to hear overlap, a spark for rare and rapid change is unleashed. But speaking our truth and expecting others to automatically hear it can be all energy and little clarity.

I often think about the many times I complained or thought about voters who vote against their self-interest. Or people who can't see what's good for them. Or someone who just doesn't get it. When confronted with my inability to convince others to rally to my specific call to action, I have often criticized the listener, completely skipping past the possibility that I may not be speaking in a language they can understand.

As I got deeper into the work, I began to wonder, *What would it look like to speak to be heard?* I discovered one way to be heard is to keep your listener as the hero of their own story.

One of the best examples I have seen of this is from Taylor Swift's open letter to Apple in 2015. Apple tried to promote its new streaming service, Apple Music, by offering it free of charge to customers for a trial period, during which they would not compensate artists. Well, Taylor would have none of it. She withheld her megahit album *1989* from Apple Music. To explain why, she penned an open letter urging the company to change its policy. She called Apple "one of my best partners," "historically progressive and generous," and an "incredible company" led by "ingenious minds." She shared her "love, reverence, and admiration for everything else Apple has done." She acknowledged that Apple was "working towards a goal of paid streaming" and that this was "beautiful progress."

Then she continued, "Three months is a long time to go unpaid, and it is unfair to ask anyone to work for nothing." She called on the leadership of Apple to change their policy. "We don't ask you for free iPhones," she concluded. "Please don't ask us to provide you with our music for no compensation."

Within days of Taylor's open letter, Apple changed its policy and agreed to pay artists whose songs were streamed by users in the free trial period. I am sure much of this change of policy was driven by Taylor's power in the music industry and the incredibly negative press her letter caused for Apple.

But Taylor made it relatively easy for Apple to change its mind. She spoke to Apple's values—"ingenious," "progressive," "generous." Her critique was that Apple's policy was a betrayal of what made it such a good company.

A different critique—one that lambasted Apple for its greed and callous disregard for struggling artists—might have pushed the company into a defensive posture. It might have led Apple to dig in its heels, making claims that its policy was in furtherance of good aims for the music industry. But even as Taylor criticized Apple's policy, she gave it points on what it had already built, focusing on nudging the company to the high road it already claimed, acknowledging the positive sense of corporate self. By doing that, Taylor's letter made it easy for her criticism to be heard.

Philosopher Kwame Anthony Appiah teaches another way to be heard by those who disagree with us. He calls it "sidling up to difference." Appiah recounts a story from the British television show *Skins*. In this show, a white English kid who happens to be gay is best friends with a young Pakistani boy from a conservative Muslim family. When the English kid shows up at his best friend's birthday party, he doesn't enter the home because his friend faltered on his promise to tell his family he was gay. "Finally, the father comes outside," Appiah tells us, and asks why his son's best friend won't come in for the party. "Your son won't tell you that I'm gay." The father pauses and then says, "You know, Islam means a lot to me, and when I go to mosque on Fridays, it's one of the great moments in my week. But I don't understand everything. One thing I do understand is that you're my son's best friend, so please come in."

Appiah points out, "He didn't say it's OK; he didn't say Islam is wrong; he didn't say Islam permits this. He said, 'You're my son's best friend and you have to come to the party.'" Sometimes, the best way to be heard is to get as close as possible without direct confrontation. Sometimes "sidling up to difference" brings both parties to a place of honest meeting.

Appiah adds, "Sometimes people think that . . . the only way to deal with these big differences between religions or around moral questions is to . . . face up to the difference directly. But I think often, as it were . . . sidling up to it is better." When disagreeing about religion, he continues, "you don't talk about religion most of the time. You talk about soccer or you talk about rock music or whatever it is you have in common as an interest."

Claudia Rankine, the American poet and philosopher who writes frequently about racial justice, has another way of speaking to be heard. She recounts the story of flying to rural Massachusetts to give a commencement speech at a local college. Her driver from the airport was a white working-class woman. This driver spoke proudly of her support for Trump. Instead of getting into an argument, Rankine asked why. This driver unloaded stories about struggling to make it in America and about the crushing weight of doctors' bills even with the Affordable Care Act health insurance. Only when this driver had become a whole person in front of Rankine's eyes—not just a caricature of a rural white voter—could Rankine engage in a meaningful way. She sums up this story by sharing that in the work of racial justice, in speaking across lines of difference, "I spend a lot of time thinking about, how can I say this so that we can stay in this car together, and yet explore the things that I want to explore with you?" Sometimes to be heard, to narrow the tough fissures that lie between us, we need to gently approach the conflict askance and explore with generosity and respect whether there is another way in, a way that keeps us each in the same car together—at the same table—as we hold the difficult tension before us just long enough for it to begin to buckle and melt.

To do this—whether to center listeners as the heroes of their story, or sidle up to difference, or start a conversation in a way that keeps listeners in the car with us—requires we first lean into curiosity. We can't do any of this without a rudimentary understanding of who we are working with—what language they speak, who they believe themselves to be, and how they see themselves fitting into the world around them. That is why seeking first to understand can be so important.

Greg Boyle once said, "I used to shake my fist a lot; I eventually learned that shaking one's fist at something doesn't change it. Only love gets fists to open." To be understood, we first have to listen to—and love—those whom we are trying to change. To be understood, we first have to understand. Not everything. Not perfectly. But enough to get us started moving toward the other person with respect and clarity.

For those of us who have stood outside the circles of power, we can bristle at the charge to speak so that the powerful may hear us. After all, for many of us, our lives are about orienting ourselves to dominant groups. We are constantly told to make people in power feel comfortable, to not rock the boat, to speak their language. Women are coached to speak in a way that men will hear them. Those who are disabled are encouraged to engage those who are able-bodied without affronting their ableism. People of color are too often asked to adapt their language to make white people comfortable. This can be enraging. And yes, it's time that those from dominant groups learn to speak other languages, that they try to adapt to others' needs. After all, how can we ever change the dominant structures that oppress others if we are constantly upholding the language and worldviews that undergird those dominant groups?

As I write, the Defund the Police movement has captured much of our national attention. For many people, the core of the debate over what role policing should play in public safety has been supplanted by a meta-debate over the usefulness of the phrase *defund the police.* Many of us have stopped wrestling with the issue at hand and have begun to debate how we should debate the issue.

At my organization, we surveyed one thousand stakeholders on a range of criminal justice reform issues. The *defund the police* slogan was considered very controversial, especially for older voters, in a way that the language around increasing funding for public health and decreasing funding for police militarization were not. *Defund the police* was not reaching the majority of voters, inspiring them to push for more limited policing. As an effort to seek to be heard, *defund the police* wasn't working. That said, the call to *defund the police* has real value. While it may not help build a broad base coalition for policy change immediately, it is a powerful rallying cry for those who have been marginalized by policing in America. For communities who have been victims at the hands of aggressive, racially motivated harm, asserting "defund the police" has real power. It is a bold-faced acknowledgment that police have caused real harm. It is a claim of power by those who have traditionally had little power at the hands of police. "This is our truth," Defund the Police activists might share. "We are powerful enough not simply to push back against police but to demand their elimination." Such a resonant claim calls out to those who have experienced similar harms. It tells them they are seen and invites them to join in a collective struggle for a safer and more just future.

And while *defund the police* might not change the hearts and minds of the median voter as some strategists hoped, it does energize and empower those who have been beaten down, those whose communities have lost precious lives to police violence. And the world is better off when those whose truth has been denied can speak their truth in public and direct ways.

There are times when we owe it to ourselves and our community to shed the burden of speaking in a language that makes others comfortable. We deserve to be honest with ourselves and each other. We honor the power of sending a clear and compelling signal to our compatriots— we see you, we value you, and you deserve to speak your truth. Over time, this insistence on speaking honestly from our own experiences in our own words can force dominant groups to reckon with the rights and experiences of marginalized groups. It can shatter the assumptions that the only language that matters is the language of those who hold power. Speaking one's truth might not change hearts and minds in the moment, but over time it can chip away at the language wielded by the powerful that denies the experiences of those excluded by that language.

Right now, I am in the midst of a multiyear-long project to work with current and former sex workers as we seek to decriminalize sex work in Illinois. At the urging of one of my board members, who herself is a former sex worker, we began by simply listening. In focus groups and interviews with sex workers, we sought to learn their experiences— why they got into sex work, what they liked about it, what they were afraid of, what type of future they imagined for themselves and others in the work. Currently, we meet regularly with about twenty members of our Sex Worker Advisory Group to map out the way forward to a state where sex workers are not criminalized.

We recently commissioned a poll of Illinois voters to determine their views on sex work. A lot of what we learned was daunting. There is a path before us to decriminalize sex work—and empower and respect sex workers while keeping them safe—but we face a wall of assumptions, stigma, and disdain for sex work and those who engage in it.

As we have begun to wrestle with what this means for how we message a campaign to make sex work legal, I have sought to find a way for our coalition to understand this a little better. Here's an analogy I offered: Take all the messages that are authentic to you about why we should decriminalize sex work—all the messages that resonate with you and that speak to your true experiences, your hopes and dreams for the future. Then take all the messages that resonate with voters, that convince them to abandon our current punitive laws for sex work.

Once we have all these messages on the table, we find the ones in the overlap. That is where we stay. For my part, I won't ask our coalition members to use messages that change the hearts and minds of voters but don't ring true to their beliefs and experiences. Similarly, I ask the coalition to set aside messages that may be powerful for them if it won't move voters or, worse, moves voters away from a position that advocates for sex workers' rights.

When our words bear the greatest possibility for change, they both hold our truth and are spoken in a language that can be understood by those for whom our truth is still foreign. To be honest, finding this overlap takes time and sometimes may not be possible. But if among our goals is seeking change and conversation around that change, working to build a common language that is both authentic to us and resonates with others can be the key to transformative change.

When you do speak, I hope you begin by being clear to yourself what you most want to accomplish. If you want to be heard by others but speak only in a language you can discern, you fail your purpose. Similarly, if you want to give crisp and clear voice to your truth but translate this so that new audiences can hear it best, you may be unable to rally your compatriots and fail to force a reckoning with your most honest experiences.

There is no right answer here. No one else can direct your purpose here, and your aims will change from context to context. But knowing *why* you speak *before* you speak is the starting call of the work. When you are clear in that answer, you can move forward with purpose and commitment, able to accomplish what you set out to do.

6

Just Ask

Perhaps it sounds obvious to you, but it took me a long time to accept that I can't just make people act on behalf of change. Because so much of my work has been focused on getting people to take action—to learn a new skill, to give money, to vote—my idea of success was tied up for so long in my ability to get others to say yes. If I made the ask just right, I thought, I would get the result.

And this is how I have often looked at the success of others. Victorious candidates win because they can garner support from influential people and voters. Smart leaders build strong organizations because they are strategic in getting customers—or, in the nonprofit world, donors—to give them money.

So much of the work includes making asks of others. Maybe it's asking for donations for a PTA fundraiser. Maybe it's knocking on doors and asking people to vote for our favorite candidate. Maybe it's asking for someone to volunteer with us. And that ask can be daunting. Because often underlying that fear of the ask is the belief that if we are good enough and smart enough—if we make the ask just right—then the other person will say yes. We often believe it all hinges on us.

But believing this ignores the complexity and human agency of the person on the other side of the ask, including that person's deep life story and how that influences their worldview, their incentives, and their likelihood to act. That deep life story is far more influential in determining whether they will act than how we ask them.

Thinking of success as depending solely on our ability to convince others to act also holds real danger. We can focus less on our purpose and our goals and become more obsessed with developing our perceived brilliance or persuasiveness or charisma. But brilliant, persuasive, and charismatic people don't always achieve their desired impact, at least right away. Rosa Parks was forty-three when she was first arrested in the Montgomery bus boycott, nearly thirteen years after she was first elected as the secretary of the local branch of the NAACP. Sometimes early success is followed by periods of intense failure. Steve Jobs founded Apple only to be fired nine years later. And sometimes people aren't even successful until after they die. Vincent van Gogh only sold one painting during his lifetime.

So if this is all true—if we can't make others do what we want and if others' life experiences influence their likelihood to do something more than our approach to them does—what does that mean? Why even bother trying to influence them to act?

Because we are social creatures trying to do big things. And that requires the participation of others. If we need others, we have to ask them. And when we acknowledge that we can't command their action—that our excellence alone is not what will compel them to do what we want— we are freed up to be bold in our approach. After all, their participation is not about us—or in reality, it is only a little about us. It's mostly about them and how we might partner together for change. So beginning with an invitation puts the focus on the work. Not on us or our shame or our brilliance.

In the decades of trying to inspire people to work alongside me for change, I have sought to keep the following key principles in mind.

Accept Mutuality

When asking someone to support your efforts, remember you are inviting them to make their own lives better. You are not begging for their beneficence. You are not a supplicant for their charity. You are doing great things in the world. Maybe you are a candidate for office trying to pass more just laws. Or you are a nonprofit leader trying to make the world a kinder and gentler place. Or you are a parent organizer trying to make the local school stronger. You absolutely need the support and partnership of others to pull it off. When you ask for someone's support, you are offering them a chance to live their values and help make the world around them better. You are proposing a partnership between someone who wants to do good and has resources—time or money or talent—and someone who is working to do good and needs these resources. That is mutuality.

I have spent decades raising money and watching fundraisers new to their career approach prospective donors timidly, hat in hand (figuratively), hoping the donor would deign to throw them some money so that they could do the work. Or diminishing themselves to gain agency: "I know you are busy; thank you so much for your time." Or beginning as though asking is a burden rather than an invitation, with lines like, "Would you mind doing ABC?" rather than understanding that what's on offer is something profound.

Approaching such prospective donors so hesitantly fails to acknowledge that asking others to join in work you both care about is a mutually beneficial proposition. The recipient gets the donations to fuel their work. The donor gets to help bring about meaningful change even though they can't do so directly themselves.

The person you ask may say no. But the prospect of them declining your invitation to join you in your efforts doesn't mean you aren't offering them something great.

Make the Ask in Their Language

I was on a short flight from Los Angeles to San Francisco once. My seat was a row or two from where the flight attendants gathered in the galley. It was so close I could overhear their conversation. The gate agent's passenger count was off by one name, and the flight attendants were trying to track down this outstanding passenger to confirm he was actually on board. Into the PA system, one of the attendants called his name repeatedly, asking that if anyone on the flight had that name to please identify themselves. No one did. Finally, and I am not sure exactly how, they found him. As he came to the front of the plane, it became clear he didn't speak English very well. It helped explain why he didn't recognize the anglicized version of his name being called out over the loudspeaker. With the help of a translator, his situation was resolved. One of the flight attendants turned to the other in frustration and said, "He doesn't speak English. That's why he didn't understand his name."

It takes a special kind of hubris to believe that as a stranger, we know how to pronounce someone's name better than they do. While few of us would be so bold to do so, we often make requests of people in our own language, not the language of the person we are asking. We use language that speaks to our needs and benefits, not their interests and motivations.

Learning from master community organizers over the years, whenever I approach someone with an ask, I try to ask myself a few questions first:

1. What is this person's story of self? Or how are they the hero of their own story?
2. What do they care about?
3. What motivates them to act?

What I love about these questions is that they force you to center the ask on the person you are approaching, not on you. It pushes you to wrestle with their wants, needs, and life story. It gets you out of your head—your own wants, needs, and life story. Inviting someone to join you in your work, and getting them to say yes, means approaching them with the respect to sit with them surrounded by the noise and joy of their own life and point out a path forward together.

Imagine you are trying to assemble a team of parent volunteers to chaperone a field trip to the art museum. You could approach your fellow parents with an ask like "We really need ten people to help the day run smoothly. Without enough volunteers, we'll have to cancel the field trip. Do you think you could help out?" I imagine you've been approached with an ask like that a thousand times in your life.

But now imagine if the ask is made something like this: "We are pulling together a team of ten parents to make the field trip to the art museum possible. Given how much you care about the class, I thought you would be perfect for this. Would you want to join us in making sure the children have an amazing experience at the art museum?" This ask is a lot harder to turn down. Sure, there are details to work out, and in the end you might not be able to do it, but this ask centers the request in your worldview. It helps you to see how saying yes might affirm your goals and values.

To make the most effective asks in someone's own language, you have to know them well. This is where seeking first to understand comes in. The more you have taken the time to learn about the person you are approaching, the more likely you will be to make the right ask of them in the right way.

But you don't have to intimately understand the deepest parts of their soul to make a solidly decent attempt at this. You can lean on what you do know of someone. You can appeal to shared experiences. You can assume a joint commitment to the institutions and causes you both spend time working with. In short, you don't have to be perfect to try to make the ask in the person's language. You just have to make a good-faith attempt. That's the work.

This approach is not meant to be transactional or Machiavellian. When you go to a café in Mexico City and ask for a cup of coffee in Spanish, you are not being manipulative. You are merely acknowledging that to get what you want, you need to make the ask in a way that the waiter can understand. To do so, you have to appreciate their language and try to ask in a way that honors that language. Acknowledging that the person you are asking has a set of interests and needs that you are making an honest attempt to address will go a long way.

Follow Up

A lot of people think the secret to raising money or amassing a cohort of volunteers or turning out persuaded voters is a brilliant strategy or an incredibly inspiring pitch. Don't get me wrong—those are incredibly helpful, but they get you nowhere without good follow-up.

Even incredibly kind people who care about the projects you are working on are incredibly busy. They have work priorities and family demands. Just because someone doesn't respond to your first phone call or email doesn't mean they won't get on board. At my current organization, even our most consistent supporters have to be asked two or three times before they will renew their donation or sign up for a volunteer shift. It's not that they don't care about our work. They just have a lot of competing priorities and need us to keep reaching out to them until they get it done.

Some people worry that follow-up can come off as pestering or rude. But when I follow up, I think of it as being "pleasantly persistent." By reaching out consistently, I am signaling to the other person that the work I am doing matters and their potential partnership is important to me. When I reach back out, they are aware that I consider the effort—the work—important for both of us.

For a few years, I led a team of community organizers who worked to get teachers and former teachers more civically active. When each organizer began in their role, they had to meet with well over a hundred community members very quickly to get a sense of the needs and wants of the community. The advice I often gave these team members, which one of them called the "one-two-three punch," was to email them first requesting a meeting. At the end of the email, I encouraged them to say something like "I know you must be incredibly busy. If I don't hear from you in a few days, I'll call you to see if we might set up a meeting." If the person didn't want a call, they had the chance to reply by email. But if there was no email, a team member would call and leave a message. In that message they would say, "If you don't have a chance to call me back in a few days, I'll text you to see if we can set something up." If they didn't hear back in a few days, they would text. If the community member didn't reply to any of the communication—three outreaches in usually two weeks—they may have been too busy to meet or just not interested right then. But this approach let them know that my team members valued them enough to follow up multiple times and in multiple ways. It also allowed them the chance to communicate in the medium they felt most comfortable with—email, phone, or text.

It's part of the work. You can do this—you can accept mutuality, you can make the ask in their language, and you can follow up persistently—and still get told no. Don't let fear stop you before you even make the ask. The work, the cause, is bigger than that.

Remember, it is not your job to tell you no. Stay in your lane. Make the ask and let the other person decide how to respond. Offer the person the opportunity to join you in a cause that will enrich their lives. Let them say yes or no. They'll do their job just fine. You don't need to do their job for them.

And if we get the no, remember that the work is about showing up for the ask, for the follow-up, and for the deep belief in a cause. That person's answer tells us so much more about them than it does about us. It is informed by how busy they are, their interests, their openness to new ideas, even their mood at that moment. Avoid the assumption that a no means a certain thing or is personal. The more appropriate and humbler response is to acknowledge that the ask was not the right opportunity for them at this time. Move on.

That doesn't mean we don't learn from a response. Early on in my career, I learned that a no could be the gateway to a yes. When someone important to my efforts told me no, I respected it and saw it as an opportunity to learn more about them. "Is this not a project you are interested in, or is it just that the timing isn't right for you?" I might ask. Or I might say, "I'd love to come back to you in a few months and give you an update on how things are going. Are there things you'd like to hear then that might make you more interested in getting involved at that point?" I didn't ask these questions of everyone, just the people I felt might get involved and whose support could be meaningful. This helped me turn their *no* today into a *yes* tomorrow.

We can learn from a series of rejections, though. If enough of the people important to our project decline, that is a great opportunity to step back and think about it. Is the project not feasible or inspiring? Could I improve how I am asking people to get involved? This is a chance to have close friends and trusted advisers give input.

One person's no isn't worth getting all that worked up about. And depending on the project, even dozens or hundreds of people's no is rarely worth getting all that worked up about, even that rare person who wants to tell you all the reasons your idea is stupid or your ask was disrespectful. The last person's rejection or disrespect shouldn't prevent you from offering the next person the opportunity to work with you to have an impact on the world around them.

Among all life on this planet, we are a species rare in our ability to collaborate toward a common purpose. When we do, amazing things are possible, almost magical things. We have ended plagues and built cities. We have launched ourselves into space and walked on the moon.

But accomplishing anything of worth, big or small, requires us to join with each other. And the first step is the ask. The ask is a key ingredient to every great accomplishment in human history. That thing so many of us find daunting, annoying, and exhausting is actually our inheritance. It is the key that makes all great things possible.

So just do the work. Do it poorly and roughly. Make the ask—over and over again as needed. And at the end of the day, let go of what any one person says in response. Allow the gap to be covered by grace. And marvel at what may become of it.

7

Ignore the Cheers and Shouts

To become great, society tells us, we must seek out criticism. Conventional wisdom teaches us that by learning from our failings, by identifying and correcting our errors, we can eventually master our craft and achieve unparalleled success. These sources of feedback are wide and far-reaching, and we'll never run out of people willing to give us teachable moments to discern our flaws or hear how we can be or do better.

As you might surmise, I find the usefulness of widespread criticism limited, believing it is rarely motivating and often unhelpful.

First of all, criticism often tells you more about those issuing "insight" than those receiving it. When we leave ourselves open to accepting the value of criticism from anyone anywhere anytime, we actually get lost in a swamp of others' insecurities, opinions, value systems, and perspectives. Being an open receptacle to all forms of critique opens us to don all the flaws and foibles hoisted on us by others.

We are unique in the world. Our particular blend of talent and life experiences is rare and flourishes with support. Listening too intently to the wide array of critical voices, we can actually drown out our own voice, powerful in its singularity. As civil rights activist Brittany Packnett Cunningham teaches us, "Every time I contort myself to fit someone else's standards, I'm insulting my creator."

Also listening too deeply to the criticism of strangers, or even of well-meaning acquaintances, runs the risk of convincing us that there is a perfect way—read: another person's way—to do our work. And this belief in some attainable ideal can stop us from moving forward or sometimes even prevent us from beginning the work in the first place. Consider with me, how many times have we assumed we couldn't try something because we weren't good enough at it to begin with? How many times have we looked around at the *New York Times* best-selling authors, or civil rights icons, or fabulously charming conveners and felt we failed to measure up, discouraged from even starting to try?

Anne Lamott stares down this inaction rooted in the fear of failing. "I think perfectionism is based on the obsessive belief that if you run carefully enough, hitting each stone just right, you won't have to die," she tells us. "The truth is that you will die anyway . . . that a lot of people who aren't even looking at their feet are going to do a whole lot better than you, and have a lot more fun while they're doing it."

I believe that the work, and our unique contribution to it, deserves our failed and imperfect attempts. By fretting too much about our own potential for failure and harsh judgment from others, we ignore the real chance that our work could make the world a brighter, fairer, more beautiful place, starting where we are.

Yes, criticism and feedback have their place. To improve our ability to do the work, we need to learn how to get better, and other people can be some of our best teachers. But the work calls us to be judicious in whose criticism we pick up. Over the years, in accepting feedback, I've landed on three questions about the person offering advice: Are they an expert? Do they care about my well-being and success? Are they offering an important perspective that is otherwise missing in my work?

Are they an expert? Society is full of Monday-morning quarterbacks. Because so much of the work happens in plain sight, almost everyone feels they have a valuable perspective to offer. How many people who have never run a campaign have an opinion about how someone should run a campaign? How many people who have never given a speech have an opinion about how to speak in public? How many people who have never had to make the hard choices in leadership have an opinion about how to govern or lead a business or a school? If you haven't done the work, if you haven't suffered failures, learned hard lessons, and gotten better in the area in which you offer judgment, I have little time for your opinions. Or as Brené Brown says, "If you're not in the arena also getting your ass kicked, I'm not interested in your feedback."

Am I in relationship with them? If you don't care about helping me succeed, why should I care about your opinion? Too many people offer feedback from the point of view of wishing the object of their critique would fail or be tempered by their imperfection, keeping them down. Cable TV is full of pundits lobbing criticism at leaders whose every stumble is reported with glee. Their assessment of what a leader of a country or an individual in justice work could be doing better is rarely of interest to me. When it comes to advice offered to me, if you have not taken the time to get to know me and work with me, your input holds little stock for me. On the other hand, if you have demonstrated to me that you care about me as a person—regardless of my wins or losses in the moment—if you have shown me that you want me to succeed in making the world around me a little bit better, then I am open to hearing what you have to say because that earned feedback helps me grow to do the work better.

Do they offer an important and different perspective? In a world where judgment comes at us fast and harsh, we tend to insulate ourselves with people who think and act just like us. After all, a small community of compatriots who have the same values, the same lived experiences, and the same reactions can buoy us in times of conflict. But bringing about change in a diverse community requires coalition-building and growing movements beyond our narrow inner circle. Being open to learning from those who offer an important viewpoint that is new and different from the ones that surround us every day helps us improve in the work. The best leaders actively work to cultivate diverse teams of advisers who can bring forth feedback grounded in a shared hope for change and in deep care for each other. If you don't have that team around you, go out and build that team. Without it, you may be forced to learn the valuable lessons from different perspectives offered by people who do not hold a deep commitment to you and your success.

For someone to offer me critical feedback I can learn from, I don't necessarily need them to be a yes on all three questions. But being a yes on at least one or two of these helps weed out the noise. And when someone brings all three, I am most open to learning from and with them.

A few years back, I began to consider becoming a school district superintendent. I wanted to explore a new model of district leadership where a superintendent could build the political capacity of parents and teachers to demand better from their school district and their state. I wanted to try this out in a medium-sized school district because I thought large urban districts were too complex to start experimenting with this new model.

I sought out a nationally esteemed training program that had a strong track record of preparing people to become superintendents of large school districts. In a pre-application interview, I asked the director of the program if they would be open to my unique vision for school district leadership. She assured me they would. I went ahead and applied.

I was invited to Los Angeles for a daylong intensive group interview. This interview was amazing. It was filled with accomplished fellow candidates from around the country. The exercises were challenging and interesting. The overall design of the day was impressive. But throughout the entire day, I was asked to put myself in the shoes of a "large district superintendent" or the "state superintendent." Not once was I asked to envision myself in the type of role I had talked about with the director.

By the end of the day, I knew the program wasn't for me. And sure enough, a few weeks later, the admissions director for the program called me and told me I wasn't accepted. He then offered to set up a time to walk through their assessment of my candidacy and offer me feedback. I politely declined. I deeply respected these leaders and the program they had designed. But it was clear their feedback wasn't for me. First, they weren't experts in the new type of superintendency I wanted to explore in a medium-sized district. Second, we weren't in relationship beyond this application process. Third, their perspective as a preeminent training ground for large district superintendents wasn't a perspective I needed at that time. While I am sure their feedback would have been insightful and grounded in lots of data, ultimately it didn't meet my criteria for useful advice. So I gave myself permission to decline the opportunity to accept their feedback.

And, yes, who doesn't love praise? Who isn't motivated by hearing we gave a knockout speech or wrote something really great or achieved a policy win others thought was too difficult? I am guilty of relishing praise like this. I live and work in the world where I'm aware I need the support of others to achieve big, bold things. I can't go it alone. When others praise me and my work, I feel successful. I feel good at my work. I feel capable of winning again in the future.

But here's the thing: If I accept people's praise as a sign of my work's quality, I have to accept their criticism. If I am willing to feel good about myself and my work when others lavish their adoration on me, I have to be willing to feel crappy about myself when they tell me I failed. Relying on others to justify my work isn't a single-sided coin.

This is what comedian Amy Poehler calls wanting the "pudding." She writes and performs her comedy without thought of whether it will be nominated for any awards. When the awards nominations roll in—as of my writing this, she has been nominated for twenty Primetime Emmys and three Golden Globes—she doesn't allow herself to get caught up in the moment. But as the awards ceremony looms, she starts thinking how great it would be to win. The award—the "pudding"—becomes something she slowly starts to crave. "You spend weeks thinking about how it doesn't matter, it's all just an honor," she writes, "and then seconds before the name of the winner is announced, everything inside you screams 'GIVE ME THAT PUDDING!'"

But when she loses, she is crestfallen. On that awards night, sitting in that audience in that fancy dress, the award has this oversized power over her. Amy Poehler is super cool and amazingly wise, but I wonder if in the brightness of that spotlight of public judgment she temporarily ceded control over whether she was proud of her work to others. I am not as cool as Amy Poehler, but I can imagine how difficult that space is—what would I have been willing to exchange in the moment? And what a poor trade-in that would be: one's own deep, abiding sense of whether one's work is good for the cheap shine of others' praise.

So if we want to avoid the sting of criticism from those who don't meet our criteria for accepting advice, we also need to be willing to walk away from the glow of praise. Two sides of the coin. This does not mean we don't appreciate praise, especially when it comes from people we respect a great deal. It simply means that we work hard to derive our own sense of worth and pride in our work from our own well-honed rubric. We remain grounded in our values, our commitment to justice honed from our deep experience and the feedback given to us by those who meet the criteria we have for accepting such feedback. We don't hand over the keys to the "judgment machine" to the unruly mob, even if they tempt us with a bright and shiny object.

My husband and I have a little trick we use to support each other when good things happen. We praise the praiser for having good taste. When he made partner at his firm, I told him how proud I was of his firm for recognizing his leadership. When I receive a good review of my work, he tells me how proud he is of that person for recognizing how good I am at what I do. It may sound silly, and we do it with a bit of tongue in cheek. But we do it consistently, clear with each other that the praise of others is not what fuels our pride in each other. I am proud of him for how hard he works, for how much he cares about giving his clients good and fair representation, for how deeply he works to take care of his team. When others notice, I am happy they notice—good on them. But whether they notice or not has no impact on my pride in my husband. No group of lawyers, no judge, and no client holds the measure or the keys of value to tell me how proud to be of him.

Ultimately, our failures and our successes do not signal our worthiness. They are simply signs that our work and the assessments of others overlap.

Remember Frederick Buechner's line: "The place God calls you to is the place where your deep gladness and the world's deep hunger meet"? What if instead of trying to win the adoration of others, we simply tried to be faithful to what we are each uniquely called to do? We work hard, we get better at something, we fail, and we improve. At the end of the day, whether we were worthy of the work has little—nothing—to do with whether others lavish us with praise or scorn.

What if we modeled our work instead after Parker Palmer's guiding question of whether we are "faithful" to our own gifts and the needs of those around us? What if we just accepted that someway, somehow, our talents and drive offered rare succor to the needs and pain of the world we live in? What if instead of trying to be praiseworthy, we just tried to be faithful to what we had to offer?

"Lighthouses don't go running all over an island looking for boats to save," Anne Lamott writes, "they just stand there shining." When a boat stumbles into the light and is spared the rocky shore, the lighthouse is no more or less shiny. It just is. When its light and the boat's need come together, the boat's crew lifts up song for the lighthouse. But the crew's appreciation does not make the lighthouse any brighter.

What if you and I refuse to make the trade? What if we walk away from the bargaining table that says we can only feel good about our work if others tell us to feel good about it? What if instead we accept that we are worthy regardless of our successes or failures at any given time? Maybe we could just live into what novelist John Steinbeck teaches us: "And now that you don't have to be perfect, you can be good."

8

Fighting Our Friends

I think the stories we learn as kids get it wrong. There are the good guys, they tell us, grounded in virtue and united in conviction. On the other side are the bad guys, diametrically opposed in values and temperament. In these cartoons and fairy tales, the fight is ultimately between the good guys and the bad guys. In order for the good guys to win, they focus all their combined energy on defeating the bad guys.

But in my life, most of the energy and time has not been spent fighting the other side. It has been a fight between the kinda good and sometimes good, between my side and also my side.

A few years ago, I was in a fight with a large civil rights group about the future of a coalition we were both in. We argued over who should be at the table and about how ambitious our work should be. In the midst of this, I embarked on a two-day road trip around the state with my colleague Anthony. As we drove, I unloaded, complaining about the friction caused by the civil rights group, saying that if we worked together and not at odds with one another, we could accomplish so much more.

Anthony listened calmly and supportively and finally said, "You complain about this conflict like it is a distraction from the real work. I think this conflict is the real work." In the fight for marriage equality, he reminded me, the bulk of the work wasn't going after the rabid opponents of marriage equality. The bulk of the work had been trying to move allies of the LGBTQ+ community who were often too scared to support us publicly, who instead often stood on the sidelines.

For much of my career in activism, every time I ended up in conflict with a friend, I panicked. I worried I had done something wrong. Or I imagined they were a terrible person bent on obstructing the work. I wasted a lot of mental space and emotional energy worrying about these fights. At my worst, I assumed that fights with friends meant that I shouldn't, or couldn't, continue in the work.

In 1963, Martin Luther King Jr. began a campaign of marches and sit-ins to protest racial segregation in Birmingham. He was arrested after a week of activity and housed in the Birmingham City Jail. While in this jail, he read an open letter issued by eight white Alabama clergymen criticizing the role of "outsiders" in tackling the city's racial tensions with unrest. While these clergymen called for "a new constructive and realistic approach to racial problems," they admonished those who sought to take to the streets to pursue a solution.

In response, King penned his powerful "Letter from a Birmingham City Jail." As you likely know, the letter is a sermon to the "white moderate." He doesn't direct his arguments to those whom he knows oppose him outright. It is not the bigoted sheriff, the racist Klan member, the racial pandering politician to whom he writes. No, he writes to those who ostensibly share his bigger-picture commitment to racial equality and harmony. It is written to, if not his friends, his potential allies who remain seated on the sidelines. "I have almost reached the regrettable conclusion," he writes, "that the Negro's greatest stumbling block in his stride toward freedom is not the White Citizen's Councilor or the Ku Klux Klanner, but the white moderate . . . who constantly says 'I agree with you in the goal you seek, but I cannot agree with your methods.'"

A more recent example can be found in political campaigns. Leading up to the presidential election of 2020, a full fourteen months elapsed between the first debate and the Democratic convention. In contrast, the time between the conventions and election day was only three months. In this era of intense vitriolic campaigning, candidates spend most of their time trying to beat out people of their own party. I saw in that campaign what I've seen in my own work. Most of campaigning is actually about fighting your friends.

Rarely do I lose sleep rehashing fights with my opponents on the other side of the ideological net. I don't work myself up on my morning commute or in the shower imagining prospective arguments with my enemies. But conflicts with my compatriots? Ooh. How I wish I could reclaim even half the time I've lost obsessing about fights with my friends.

Why We Fight Our Friends

Our allies matter so much. We want the same outcomes, and we share the same values or most of them. So why in the world do we fight our friends?

First, oppressive systems lie to us. They try to convince us that there is not enough to go around. There is not enough money, not enough seats at the table, not enough credit for work well done. If decision makers will only sit down with the most powerful among us, we better take power away from others and hoard our own power to ensure we are always at the table. If grant money will only go to the most successful among us, we better appear like we did it all. If many do the work but only a few are praised publicly, we better elbow others out of the way to make sure we are out in front when accolades are distributed. Why do we fight our friends? We fear scarcity.

When you face the prospect of fighting your friends, it is important to see this is how unjust systems work. Once you do, you realize that when you fight your friends in the pursuit of influence, money, or public affection, you are doing the work of the oppressors. When we turn on our friends—and our friends on us—we use the tools of unjust systems against each other. And often we are unaware we are doing it. We believe we are acting for other reasons. Perhaps we act out of righteous indignation at an ally's actions. Or perhaps we act in firm belief that we are better positioned to make the decisions for the community. And while those surface-level reasons may ring true, the underlying cause of the fight is that the oppressive systems of power we live in have set us up to attack each other. And we are doing their bidding.

With what I've learned about how systems pit ally against ally, I've begun to do the work of advocacy differently. Now, when preparing to "fight" an ally, I try to ask myself this key question: If I believed resources were abundant—that money and praise and public support were not limited—would I fight?

Often the answer is no. It's both subversive and generative to refuse to accept the premise that we should fight over scraps. How liberating it is to refuse to take up the oppressor's tools.

Another reason we are so easily drawn into fighting our own allies is because they are right next to us, while our opponents are so far away ideologically and often physically. Those who benefit from oppressive systems distance themselves from those most marginalized by these systems. And the gap between the two is fraught with barriers: limited public transportation, alarm systems, gated communities, and stop-and-frisk police who often target Black, brown, Indigenous, and LGBTQ+ communities, making it difficult for those who are harmed by the system to reach and appeal to those who benefit from the system.

What privilege builds, then, is a linear model of oppression. Those who benefit most from the system are at one end, and those who are most harmed are at the other end. The rest fall in between in varying gradations of harm. Those who are most harmed can't get to or often can't even see those who are most responsible. They usually only have access to the few people in that line closest to them. When we look down the line to find those culpable, responsible for the harm, we tend to see only those nearest to us. Compared to us, they look responsible for the harm coming to our communities. So we lash out at the people closest to us in line, while those on the far end remain intentionally and systemically insulated.

A few summers ago, a group of queer activists disrupted the Chicago Pride Parade. The protestors came armed with a list of demands fueled in large part by what they saw as rampant corporate pinkwashing—the practice of using support for LGBTQ+ equality as a cover for the engagement in unjust practices toward other communities. The activists sent an open letter asserting their position: "We denounce the participation of banks and corporations in the Chicago Pride Parade that contribute to the genocide of indigenous people, the continued investment in . . . oil pipelines, and the debt crises in oppressed communities across the planet." It was a beautiful moment—a dozen mostly Black and brown trans activists and their coconspirators gathered to stop a flood of marchers to bring attention to injustices broadly and deeply felt.

Even so, many in the LGBTQ+ community were confused, while others were deeply offended. You may now know Pride parades as a joyful celebration of the queer community, full of cheering people and dancing. But the Pride parades that began in 1970 were marches of protest, commemorating the anniversary of the Stonewall riots. Pride is so important to the LGBTQ+ community because the primary tools used for so long to oppress us were shame and stigma. By refusing to internalize the shame of mainstream America, by marching in the streets openly and proudly, LGBTQ+ people push back against their own oppression in the most powerful and subversive way possible. It took decades of marches to evolve into an event with thousands of participants and a million spectators. For the biggest celebration of the LGBTQ+ community—itself a form of protest—to now be the target of another protest by allies didn't make sense to many. We were all on the same team, many thought, so why were we being targeted?

The protest had real impact. It captured the attention of spectators at a major public event and garnered significant media attention. It forced LGBTQ+ community leaders to begin asking hard questions about the relationships between our community-based organizations and corporate power. But thinking about oppressive systems as that line helps illuminate what was happening in a different way. CEOs and corporate leaders did not proactively engage the Black and brown trans activists, granting them access to the offices or homes of corporate CEOs. They did not invite these activists into shareholder convenings. They did not share the time and location of the corporate board meetings. Walled off from the inner sanctums of corporate decision-making, the activists did have access to the broader LGBTQ+ community who did have relationships with those same corporations—a parade with corporate funding and corporate participation. That meant the parade could become an access point for protesting the oppression. The parade then became—in their line of sight—the thing closest to the oppression they wanted to rail against. As CEOs and shareholders and board members were spared the protestors' rage, the LGBTQ+ marchers and spectators became the target of the protest. This is how the system often works: insulating the most powerful while allies target each other.

There's another reason we fight our coconspirators in the work. It's a function of how so many people view the struggle. The vegan professor and activist Melanie Joy warns of the risk in social justice to view all actions through the lens of our personal choices and values alone. In this frame, people assign one of three roles to every person: they are the victim, the perpetrator, or the hero. Once people are fit neatly into their role, we don't have to ask the deeper question: How did they get there? We don't have to see their actions from a nuanced lens, admitting these actions can be part right and part wrong. We can

celebrate our heroes, rage against the villainy of our perpetrators, and lay sympathy and pity on our victims. Hands
washed. Done.

But in reality, Joy reminds us, we are all products of and
actors in the systems that surround us. You can't understand meat-eating, she explains, as simply the cruel and
selfish act of cruel and selfish people. I mean you could, but
that doesn't help you get to the root of the issue. Instead,
you have to view behavior as a function of the complex
histories, incentives, social meanings, and models around
us. Good people eat meat because we are taught to do so
at an early age, it is immersed in most of our major social
traditions, and everyone around us does it. Acknowledging the power of the system to drive meat-eating
doesn't mean being fatalistic, thinking we can't effect
change. Nor does it mean giving a free pass to all actors
and all actions as the inevitable culmination of an unjust
system barreling over free choice and will. It simply means
acknowledging that if we want to understand—and ultimately change—behavior, we have to zoom out and look
at it in the broader context.

We often fight our friends because we look at too
many things from the lens of personal behavior. Anyone
who has seen an ally turn on them after they disagree
with them has experienced this role-shifting—from playing the role of a co-hero to being assigned the role of

the perpetrator. It can happen fast, and when it does, it's perplexing.

Over the years, I've had to dust off my Psych 101 textbook to remind myself of two biases that help explain why this role-shifting happens. These are biases that can wreak havoc on our work with allies. First, is the fundamental attribution error. This is the tendency we all have to blame our own shortcomings on situational factors but blame others' shortcomings on personality flaws. If I am late for a meeting, I know it is because of a train breakdown. If you are late for a meeting, I may think it is because you are disorganized or don't value other people's time.

The second bias ties right in—the confirmation bias. This bias means we search for, collect, and remember information that confirms our priors while we ignore information that challenges our priors. If I have already decided that you don't value people's time, I don't remember all the meetings you were punctual for, but I can easily chronicle the meetings you were late for.

Combine these two and you have a whirlwind of self-feeding biases that can make even the strongest friend and ally begin to look like the villain. To refuse to look at systems and context and only view things from the lens of personal behavior means we will destroy potential bonds as the twins of the fundamental attribution error and confirmation bias engage. Our friends' actions can be construed not as minor infractions or as the result of a complex system producing legitimate disagreement but as markers of their fundamental flaws. Add to that carefully curated data points, and you can harden that viewpoint until the chasm created between allies is so wide that where once friendship existed now only enmity and distrust pervade.

If agreement with us on most things becomes the primary determinant of whether we view people as good or bad—the only test being whether they share *our* values or don't—we build a minefield in which people's every step can blow up our potential bonds with them. If the only roles we are willing to assign are victim, hero, and perpetrator, disagreement with us eliminates others from the roles of victim or hero. There is only one role left for people to play. And such limited casting is hard—I'd say impossible— to build generative, cooperative relationships on.

Knowing all this—how powerful the inertia of the system is and how persuasive the biases driving us are—when confronted with a potential fight with a friend, I simply try to remember to take a pause. Don't fight the fight until it's a fight.

This is a lesson I learned most pointedly while running the education nonprofit in Los Angeles. Our organization recruited, trained, placed, and supported amazing teachers in classrooms in low-income communities. In order to do this work, we signed agreements with local school districts to hire teachers. Los Angeles Unified School District (LAUSD), being the second-largest school district in the country, regularly agreed to hire between one hundred and two hundred teachers through our efforts each year. But sure enough each spring, with over one hundred teachers planning to move to LA for a promised job, LAUSD would sometimes go soft. "Our hiring projections for the year are lower than before," they would tell me only weeks before our new recruits arrived, "so we aren't going to hire your teachers."

Not surprisingly, when a bomb like this dropped, I would reel. With the prospect of one hundred people who had accepted our offers planning to uproot their lives and move to LA only to find out they had no jobs, my first instinct was to panic. One time after getting the news of the threat of our contract being rescinded, I got up from my desk, walked to the supply closet, and lay on the floor, desperate. What was I going to do with one hundred angry, unemployed aspiring teachers? When my assistant finally found me, she peered through the cracked door and asked if I was OK. "Just give me a minute," I said. She backed away and gently shut the door.

After the panic subsided, my next instinct was to fight. I would huddle with my team and make plans to beat back the threat. I would hop on the phone and call my colleagues around the country to rage against the injustice and get ideas. I would toss and turn at night, imagining fights in which I righteously won arguments with LAUSD bottlenecks, leaving them crestfallen and me victorious. I would stand in the shower each morning and get lost in a train of thought about all the backup plans I would roll out to protect our incoming teachers if they couldn't get a job in LAUSD.

And usually, after a few days of laying the groundwork and reaching out to district leaders to begin my onslaught, the threat would disappear. Sometimes, I learned, it was simply a misunderstanding on the part of the person who delivered the news. Sometimes I just had to make a simple phone call to a well-placed ally in the district and begin asking questions for the matter to resolve. Sometimes the underlying fact pattern changed quickly, and all was fine.

All my panic and rage and righteous indignation on behalf of our incoming teachers? It did nothing. "Don't ride the roller coaster," a friend taught me. It is a waste of energy to hop on only to realize the ride itself was unnecessary.

Getting on that emotional roller coaster immediately prevented me from acting strategically. Complex problems require creative solutions. Fear and anger impede that creativity. It also made me tense and unproductive with potential partners. I would approach people with key insight to the problem's resolution, but my underlying anxiety or righteous resentment inhibited my ability to generate the trust they needed to work for a solution together. But finally, and maybe most importantly, the roller-coaster approach was unkind to myself. Focused on fear and anger, my personal life—my sleep, my time with family and friends, even my downtime—would be impeded by my preoccupation with the looming fight. And often the looming fight never came.

I eventually promised myself I would tap down the instinct to respond out of the gate in anger or threats. *Don't fight the fight until it's a fight.* Now more often, when presented with a locked door, I try everything else first before I bust through. Wiggle the doorknob, test the deadbolt, knock gently, look around to see if there is another door nearby, maybe try a window. And I tell myself that I have the fight in me if none of those works. No roller coaster, no getting worked up, no anticipating the busting through until I have first tested all the other possible ways to proceed.

How to Fight Our Friends

And, yes, no matter how aware you are of systems, of the line, of your psychological baggage, it's going to happen.

Your friends are going to lash out at you. You are going to feel the urge to rage against them. It sucks. But it's also part of the work. And there are ways to do it well. How do you step out on these mini battlefields with minimal collateral damage to yourself and your relationships?

Here's what I've learned is the key to better friend and ally fights: fight firmly, fight narrowly, and fight calmly.

Fight firmly. Own your perspective and experience. Honor it by bringing it to bear confidently in the disagreement. "Be sure you put your feet in the right place, then stand firm," Abraham Lincoln taught. This is not to say avoid compromise, fight to the bitter end unyieldingly. Rather, if you have come honestly and thoughtfully to a position that puts you at odds with a colleague—and if you have tried every reasonable way to not let it get to the fight—when you do fight, bring the fullness of your position forward unapologetically.

I have come to believe there are three types of people when it comes to dealing with conflict. Always be skeptical of those who try to boil all of humanity into a few "types," but I hope you'll bear with me on this one. Some are conflict-seeking. These are the people who are drawn to the fight. "No fight? No passion," they seem to say. These people fill my social media feed daily with passionate attacks of the unrighteous. Some are even ready to take to the streets in protest right away.

Another set are those who are conflict-avoidant. Conflict is so uncomfortable for them that they seek to avoid it at all costs. In some families, people are raised with a belief that conflict is bad, so it is so firmly ingrained in them that if they are engaged in conflict, they must have done something wrong. When they are confronted with the potential for conflict, they immediately back down—hide their truth, bury their perspectives and experiences, believing that if sharing them may lead to conflict, then these truths must be problematic.

And there are those of us who are, or who have become, conflict-tolerant. This is now where I sit, neither excitedly seeking a fight nor running away from it. When we get to the precipice of conflict, we engage in it willingly and comfortably. Some of us stand in this place through inclination; others started more conflict-avoidant or conflict-seeking and through practice learned to tack toward conflict tolerance. I see this as the strongest foundation for fighting well.

At the core of conflict tolerance is the willingness to own and unapologetically bring forth one's truth and experience. Remember that letter Taylor Swift wrote to Apple? In that letter, she wrote, "This is not about me." She continued, "This is about the new artist or band that has just released their first single and will not be paid for its success. This is about the young songwriter who just got his or her first cut and thought that the royalties from that would get them out of debt. This is about the producer who works tirelessly to innovate and create, just like the innovators and creators at Apple are pioneering in their field . . . but will not get paid for a quarter of a year's worth of plays on his or her songs."

But, of course, this was also about her. Because Taylor herself had been a "new artist" and a "young songwriter" and a "producer." Her experiences and the people she met along the way gave her important insight into how Apple's decision impacted her and the community she knew so well. She owned her experiences and perspectives honestly and with courage. And as you know, a few days after her open letter went public, Apple reversed its decision and agreed to compensate artists during the free three-month period.

Do not be afraid to speak the truth of your experiences. Do not be afraid to share the stories your compatriots have shared with you and allowed you to share. Be firm and unapologetic.

Fight narrowly. Focus on the disagreement at hand. Do not bring in the kitchen sink of disagreements and the laundry list of wrongs suffered at the hands of the other party. And don't go nuclear, trying to win all future wars in one single battle. I admit fighting narrowly in this way is a constant struggle for me. My temperament and practice over the years have helped me stay calm and seek off-ramps from the fight before it begins. So far, so good. But once I am in the fight, I can quickly be the worst version of myself. I resent being dragged into a fight, often by someone I dislike and don't respect. I see their hypocrisies and resentfully conjure up any previous slights. My distaste borders on disdain. I am righteously indignant about the fight and want to end it in such a way that this person can never drag me into a fight again. A supposed ally tries to block my work on an important issue multiple times, I want them in a room with an audience so I can draw up all the horrible hypocritical things they have done, show the world who they really are, and end their smug interference in my work for good. I can be a real asshole.

But I am afraid of this asshole I can become. The irony is that playing the loop of past harms over and over again doesn't keep the other person up at night or interfere with the other person's downtime. Like the famous adage points out, I am taking the poison and hoping the other person dies. But I also fear my tendency to go for the jugular, which forces me to bite my tongue and sometimes withdraw from active participation in an actual disagreement for fear of going too far.

Fighting narrowly, fighting well, means checking all those resentments at the door. You can always pick them up on your way out if you want. It also means accepting that there may be future fights—but those are fights you don't have to wage simultaneously with this one. Wage conflict on the disagreement at hand, no more and no less.

Fighting narrowly doesn't just mean staying focused on the disagreement at hand. It also means not broadening the fight to add others in. It means not fueling the system's impetus to have friends fight each other. An instinct I see play out in ally fights is to rally other champions to our side. When we fight our allies, we vent our frustrations to other friends in the fight. They agree with us in whole or in part, and we feel our righteousness is ratified. We repeat to others. But all this does is spread toxicity within the community. We are not working to resolve the conflict. We are merely weakening the potential bonds within the community with our discontent. This is not to say that at times we shouldn't organize people to convince someone to make different decisions—after all, this is what activism and community organizing are all about. But when we prepare to fight a friend, it is helpful to avoid amassing an army from within our community to attack our ally and a member of the community.

At the root of our drive to rally others to our side, even in a fight with friends, is often the fear that we are not enough, that our concerns are not valid unless they are ratified by others or that we will not be heard unless we bolster the strength of our voice. But how differently might we act if we truly believed we were enough? How might we break the cycle of friends fighting friends if we refused to grow the army?

When I am preparing to fight a friend, I am so tempted to unleash the vast data trove I have assembled. "It's not just me," I want to say, "everybody thinks you are a jerk." But really what I want to add is, "So you better take me seriously." When I remind myself that I am enough, though, I can let go of the shadow army of compatriots I have prepped to bring into the disagreement. After all, it really doesn't matter how many or how few people I have on my side because my experiences and perspectives in this disagreement are sufficiently valid. When I draw on this realization, I can fight narrowly.

Fight calmly. This is where it all comes together. You have entered into the fight with an understanding of how the system works and what brought allies into a fight. You have sought many off-ramps to avoid the fight. You are prepared to fight firmly, owning your truth and experiences. You will not broaden the fight to other issues or other people. So now the final piece is to accept where you are and fight calmly.

Take a breath and remember: the entire system is set up to turn us against each other. There will undoubtedly be points of real meaningful conflict between allies. But it's helpful to remember that there is a lot of noise and social pressure coming together to create the fight. When you remember this, you can begin to depersonalize the conflict.

The anger you will feel against a compatriot may have a nugget of real anger, but the system may also have piled layers of rage on top of that nugget. Maybe an ally really stepped out of line. But will part of your frustration be due to the fact that you are afraid there isn't enough good stuff to go around and that they are taking from you? Will part of your frustration be due to the fact that they are the closest thing to you who benefits from an unjust system, and it is easy to lash out at them and hold them responsible for the whole thing? Will part of your frustration be due to the fact that they have betrayed some small part of your confidence, and so now they seem like the perpetrators of injustice, not just a co-hero who made a tiny misstep?

And a fight doesn't just begin with you. When an ally rages at you, it can be easy to personalize it. After all, the anger directed at us is meant to feel personal. The context they bring up, the words they use, the actions they describe are meant to apply to no one but us. But the same systems that act on us also act on them. Maybe they are afraid you are hoarding social benefits from them, or maybe you are the closest target and someone who represents everyone who stands farther from them in the line of oppression, or they may view you as the perpetrator and themselves as the hero guarding the victims.

It's important to remember no one can control an ally's reactions. My rule is to try to give them a pass in the moment. I take a breath, try to ignore the vitriol, and respond calmly to their concern. Often the anger seems like it is about me, but it so often is not about me. Or more accurately, it is only a little bit about me. If they are still cruel and rageful a few days later, then we have a problem. But if not, we move past it. If the original treatment was particularly egregious, I'll discuss that with them later after tempers have cooled, but otherwise I just let it go.

When I am at my best, I put in check my righteous indignation of being accused, my frustration at having my expertise called into question, my basic human desire to punch back. I accept that doing work that matters—work that impacts real people—brings out reactions in people that aren't fair, but the system wants the fight. Because if we are fighting about how we are fighting, then we are not fighting together to beat the system. Remembering this helps to depersonalize the fight or maybe more accurately helps you narrow the fight to the most accurate, tiniest part of the conflict. This will let the winds out of the sails and will help you step into the battlefield calm and grounded.

Fighting calmly ultimately requires you not to stress too much about this one tussle. In almost all fights with friends, there will be many more. So try not to worry too much about this one. It will almost certainly not be the defining fight of your work.

Remember in the *Bhagavad Gita* how Arjuna is on the battlefield prepared to fight his cousins. He is distraught over anxieties and fears—fears about winning, fears about losing. The god Krishna instructs him to "fight for the sake of fighting, without considering happiness or distress, loss or gain, victory or defeat." That is what you are called to do when fighting your friends. For me, this means tamping down the voices that quicken my pulse and make me like a pile of kindling awaiting the match of the slightest provocation. There will be other days and other fights. As long as I fight well—firmly, narrowly, and calmly—I'll almost certainly be fine in the long run.

And no matter how much of an asshole they are being or you are being, leave room for the possibility—maybe now, maybe a long time from now—that this person and you may behave better. No one is a permanent, indelible version of themselves. So try not to make the fight too personal; try not to make them believe they are the greatest hypocrite and jerk of all time. They won't believe you in the moment anyway. And doing so may only burn a bridge you may need them to cross in the future.

Fighting your friends is a major part of the work.

When the time comes—if you haven't found a more productive way around the conflict and if you end up in it—fight firmly, calmly, and narrowly.

It's not easy. But that's OK. Paulo Coelho counsels us to remember that a life of peacefulness "would be a contradiction with nature." "Nature is never in peace," he reminds us. "You see the winter fighting against summer. You see the sun exploding. . . . Confrontation is a part of life."

There is no getting around it. Confrontation is not the exception to the rule. It is the rule. So engage in it the best you can. And if it goes poorly, and your potential allies in the work remain selfish, spiteful jerks, just remember to let go. This life—this work—is a long walk. There will be other fights. Treat yourself and others with kindness. Rest up for the next one.

9

We Inherit Cruelty

Dawn had barely rubbed the sleep from its eyes when I slid out on our front porch, coffee in hand, to watch the lazy waters of the Kalamazoo River change their colors in the rising morning light. My daughter, Joey, had crawled into our bed at some unchronicled hour of the night so that when I woke, she and Toby were snuggled warmly into each other. I seized the rare blessing, for I was not always an earlier riser than Joey those days. I slid out of bed and eased downstairs to grab a cup of coffee, relish a quiet home, and step out into a late-spring morning to savor the warmth.

As I walked onto the front porch, I stumbled on two dead chicks lying with dried and mottled feathers, shaking me out of my post-dawn reverie. I had seen the nest, crammed between the eave and its weight-bearing beam, a few weeks prior. The nest the now-dead chicks had called home was one of a handful of nests plugging empty spaces at the edges of our home. And the nests, along with the budding red maples and greening seagrass and daffodils blooming valiantly against the still-cold Michigan ground signaled hope and renewal for us, on our property and in our lives.

In my marriage, as in most, responsibilities are divided. Along with scheduling doctor's appointments and monitoring the family budget, I have also become the "dead bird" husband. So I placed my coffee on the front porch's bench and went off to the garage to grab the shovel I would use to scoop up the delicate bodies and toss them into the woods. I wasn't ready to explain them to my three-year-old daughter.

I don't know how these baby birds ended up lifeless eight feet below the only home they ever knew. Were they abandoned by a mother bird? Did a bird parent seek food for them and not make it back? I didn't know. But to be honest, I am not sure I want to learn the true answers. I have avoided googling "why do baby chicks fall from nests?" to guard my ignorance of the many cruelties that can befall these helpless animals. Ever since Joey came into our lives, I can't bear stories of little ones in pain, even if these little ones are animals.

What I do know is that cruelty is woven deep within the fabric of the world. The chicks' death, while a sad interruption in my otherwise content-filled morning, is not the exception. It is the rule. Our entire natural world is built on the core principle that life steals life and often in the most gruesome ways. Annie Dillard tells us that parasitic wasps, who bury their eggs deep in the bodies of living insects so that the hatching larva can secure their first meal by eating their host alive, make up 20 percent of all species. Our rural Michigan property, like the world around us, teems with beauty. But underneath the wild-flower bed, and lilac tree, and grass speckled with sunlight pouring through the broad oak leaves above is a world fighting to live by taking the lives of others.

Out of this bedrock of cruelty, our ancestors carved out human civilization. The institutions we have shaped too often echo the cruelty from which they in turn were shaped. Just as in the natural world, where life steals life, so our societies and their power structures steal and hoard benefits—wealth, opportunity, security. Into this world steeped in pain we were all born. No one we know built these learned systems that perpetuate injustice. Yet every day we wake up into a society whose oppressions were built over centuries in a world whose cruelties were honed over billions of years.

Yet I sometimes reflect with wonder on how much we have built that spits in the face of this inheritance of cruelty. We care for our young and our old. We sacrifice for the good of the group. We share and collaborate. But we have not fully escaped our past. Humanity doubles down on cruelty in thousands of ways each day.

So now what? What do we do with this knowledge?

I take two lessons from this square-shouldered acknowledgment of the world from which we grow. First, I push myself to let others off the hook just a little bit. We are all broken people living in a broken world. Every time we choose to hoard benefits, exclude others, and practice unkindness, we are merely walking the grooves the world created for us billions of years ago.

This may sound totally off. We live in a world of genocide and systemic racism and crippling poverty. For those like me—and hopefully like you—who carry a sense of justice buried deep within our bones, the last thing we think we need is to let others off the hook. After all, those who benefit most from oppressive systems do a good enough job of letting themselves off the hook. I can think of many rich white defendants who got off scot-free in our courthouses or harassers who escaped culpability in the workplace. And I can't name one titan of industry serving jail time for the 2008 financial collapse. We don't need less accountability. We need more of it. There is no justice without reckoning. There is no reconciliation without truth.

What I ask of myself, and of you too, is to see in the crimes and cruelties of others both the acts of intention and the patterns of our inheritance. To acknowledge will and inertia. I want my sternest accusations and harshest judgments to befall systems. I hope to hold a little more softness for those who act within them.

As I read the news and scroll through social media, my attention draws toward the harshest acts of global cruelty. But to be honest, I personally encounter many more smaller cruelties closer to home every day. We are all living out patterns handed down to us, perpetuating injustices as part of our normal course of being. I seek to size my disdain accurately. As I rail against the individuals whose actions form the tip of the circling fin, my aim is to see the leviathan of a world born from cruelty lurking beneath the surface, forcing the tip of individual injustice above the waterline.

I confess I write this, like so much else in this book, to not just encourage you but to remind myself to act with this wisdom and mercy. Because I so easily tilt toward anger and judgment at those I see advancing harm. I fear my instinct to assign blame when someone blocks my work for change. Or when someone defends broken and harmful systems. And I am not talking about tyrants or psychopaths here. I am talking about the everyday good-hearted allies and misguided opponents.

A decade ago, I helped lead an organization that worked to get teachers more politically active. We worked primarily with one national organization; our largest partner being also our largest funder. Our primary contact there was one of the most unique leaders I have ever worked with. She combined fierceness and gentleness in a combination I have never seen—before or since. I had known her to regularly work 80–100 hour weeks, insistent that the injustices young people of color face in our country should not be borne one day longer. She also wrapped her team in love and warmth, demonstrating deep care for them—investing in their personal needs and their professional growth.

Each year, we submitted a funding proposal to this partner organization, which this leader was charged with incorporating in her work and submitting for internal vetting on her end. It was always a stressful time. Dozens of leaders throughout her organization could critique, derail, or even defund the work of partner teams, both within and outside the organization. The leader we worked with asked me for some information about my team's work for her broader proposal. Whether I misunderstood, or thought I should give her something different, I don't remember. But whatever I supplied her with did not meet her expectations. We had been friends for nearly a decade and she picked up the phone to yell at me. "Brian, I told what I wanted. You did not do it. I expect you to get it to me now," she said forcefully and ended the call. I was shocked. I had never been yelled at before by a partner or funder. I had never been yelled at before by this leader, a friend. I was angry. I was hurt. Our relationship never recovered.

In the months and years that followed, I have earned some glimpses into her world in that moment. She was operating at a time when the work of her entire team—including our partnership—could have been defunded in any year, meaning she would have to curtail her work and layoff team members. She had to put on a dog-and-pony show each year to department heads who often were young, inexperienced, and cruel stemming from their own stress and myopia. It was not uncommon for her to be demeaned by leaders in her organization who had less experience, produced fewer results, and led smaller teams; simply because the structure of the organization allowed that. It was against this background that she lost her cool with me. I wish I had not been so caught up in my own pain that I could not to hold curiosity for the pain she must have been experiencing. Had I held more gentle space for her in that moment, I think I might have been a better partner, maybe even helping her to navigate the broken system she was operating in so that our work together could have been stronger. Maybe I could have been a better friend.

I hope in the future maybe I can hold more gentle space for others in the work as well. Maybe I can hold space for the white woman who chooses to send her kids to an expensive private school but opposes local public school options for low-income families in her city. Maybe I can hold space for the elected official who is willing to teach children about the wives of straight men in history but thinks we should hide away the same-sex partners of LGBTQ+ historical figures.

Maybe I can even hold space for myself.

At the age of twenty-eight, I struggled in my first non-profit management role. I inherited a team of nine, soon to be thirty. We had to raise three million dollars, soon to be seven million, every year just to keep the work afloat. We supported nearly four hundred teachers working in some of the toughest conditions in the city. I had never managed people, raised money, or been responsible for so many others before.

As I worked seventy to eighty hours a week—scrambling to learn how to do my job as I was doing my job—my young team suffered. They need guidance and clarity. They needed coaching and support. They needed kindness and inspiration. I couldn't even offer those things to myself, let alone to anyone else.

At one point, I had a meeting with my development director, who was particularly unhappy and struggling. Shortly after the meeting started, she began to cry. She felt unsuccessful and didn't know what to do. I sat there, stone-faced, and offered some poor attempt at consolation and direction.

After the meeting ended, the development director left the office, and I called a colleague I trusted and complained, "I know my team has emotions; I just wish they wouldn't have them with me."

What a heartless thing to believe in the face of someone breaking down in tears. And I was heartless. I wasn't cruel or malicious; I just didn't have it in me to soothe my development director, to tell her she was fine, that it was all going to be OK, and here is how we were going to make it work. I didn't have it in me to do that because I myself was barely keeping my head above water. I was exhausted and anxious and didn't know how I was going to make it through the year keeping the organization and all its people afloat. I was on empty and couldn't muster up the kindness or assurance for myself, let alone anyone else. So my team suffered, and I withdrew. In my view, there are few sins worse than denying support to those in your life who need it most.

Looking back, well over a decade later, I can see what happened with a deeper understanding and a generosity to myself and others that I didn't have in the moment. Things got better, slowly. I learned my job, grew in my confidence, and was able to establish a culture of both high expectations and deep care. But it took a few years, and most people who started with me in the beginning didn't make it to the end. They left in sadness and anger and disappointment. And I understand why.

I lacked compassion and could be downright unkind. I was a new leader with limited skills, facing daunting social injustice and a large team. These were not my fault. I did not cause these deficiencies. It would take me time to meet them head on and improve enough to give my team what they needed. Now I think that if I can hold space for others who have inherited the brokenness of their station, the least I can do is hold that same space for my team and myself.

None of us, myself included, created our unjust systems. The ignorance that enshrouds us, the limitations of our abilities, and the desire to keep what benefits us are by-products of the world we were born into. When we extend a little bit of grace and patience to ourselves and others immersed in the work but doing it badly, we acknowledge the systems at play.

Extending grace is not the same as letting go. If we stopped here, we fail to see the full picture. Because it is not just that we have inherited cruelty. We also have inherited the rare capacity to move the world toward mercy and kindness. And this is the second lesson that acknowledging the cruelty around us imparts. Cruelty may be our inheritance, but it is not our destiny.

One of the kindest people I have worked with was a man who ran a national nonprofit. A Russian immigrant who came to the States as a child, he learned English by going to English-only public schools in California and Michigan. He learned coding and started a successful software company, which he later sold. He eventually became a partner at an elite global consulting firm, advising Fortune 100 businesses how to be more profitable. One day he left, took a massive pay cut, and went to run a nonprofit getting teachers and former teachers more politically active. It was here that he ended up recruiting me to work for him.

This leader had a rule that we were never to speak ill of any other nonprofit outside our organization. He rightly saw that organizations and leaders in the nonprofit space often have to compete with each other for publicity, reputation, and ultimately funding from a limited number of donors. This scarcity mindset—fear that there is not enough money or credit to go around—can lead to sharp elbows in the field. Combine this with the ego and power of conviction required to succeed in the public sector, and nonprofit leaders can be particularly aggressive toward each other.

But my former boss would have none of it. He would sit in rooms where twenty-seven-year-old employees of partner organizations would tell him how to do his job. He would be at conferences and hear how colleagues at other nonprofits would call his work inept. He would have funders who had never worked in education or politics tell him he didn't understand how his own field worked. And yet whenever he was asked—by a donor, a reporter, or another leader—what he thought of one of these leaders who so readily maligned him, he would simply say, "The country is better when they are successful at their work. You should support them to the greatest extent possible."

It was remarkable to behold. He would suffer the slings and arrows of his peers only to turn around and champion them. He inherited the cruelty of the world around him but would not allow that cruelty to be his destiny. And this was one of his greatest contributions to our collective work. He refused to limit our broader success as a community by tearing down his colleagues. He was a true champion for all of us struggling to make our slice of the world—the schools that serve our most vulnerable students—better for all. The cooperation of his peers in this effort was nice, but he did not require it for him to bestow his support on all of them.

We are called to move beyond the brokenness we have been born into. As humans, we have been given the rare gift of being able to call creation's bluff. We see your cruelty and raise you kindness. We have been bestowed with the unique ability to create love and fairness out of chaos and life-stealing. Every time we choose gentleness in the face of anger, gratitude in the face of fear, generosity in the face of selfishness, we are leaning into our greatest calling—to take the world of cruelty we have inherited and remake it into a softer and more beautiful place.

I hope you see the small indignities of those around us for what they are—a manifestation of a world built on cruelty. Hold generosity of spirit for those who slight you, hoard your benefits, and slow the work. They are merely acting out a pattern woven deep in the fabric of the world.

Call them out.

Hold the unjust accountable.

Be angry.

But store the bulk of your rage to use against the systems that produce such cruelty, not against the players who act those systems out. Grab hold of what makes us all uniquely human, the insistence that we will not readily pass on the cruelties we have inherited. Stay true to your calling, your community, and your values and don't let your work be defined by the ugliness thrown at you. Work every day, in every interaction, to choose your better nature and make goodness and gentleness out of stern stuff.

As I cradled the second of the lifeless birds in my garden shovel, I stopped and held a gentle prayer in my heart for this once-wild and beautiful thing. I brought it far into the woods, hoping to give it a soft landing to return its body to the earth. I walked back into our home, as the sun rose behind me above the polychromatic river, and walked up the stairs to my husband and daughter. I peeked in to see them both cuddled in our bed, sheets strewn about them as they clung softly to one another breathing in tandem. I thanked God for the blessings that rise out of a world steeped in pain and went downstairs quietly to pour myself another cup of coffee.

10

Virtue and Vice

I have long hoped that my disheveled mind could be saved by a personality test. I am a sucker for a Myers-Briggs, an Enneagram, or a "What Disney prince are you most like?" Facebook quiz. I am a mix of contradictions and complexities that challenge my craving for order and simplicity.

I am forty-five years old as I write this, and I am still working to understand myself. But what I know is that there are no neat lines to be drawn. I am—we all are—unique and messy. You are on the cusp of charting your own path and probably feel this mess intensely these days. I wish I could assure you there was a sorting hat that could clearly and definitively tell you who you are and where you belong at all times. But that's just not the case.

Where this causes me the greatest confusion is in trying to order and categorize my predilections. Is my craving for routine a virtue in that it helps me create order to my day and allows me to get a lot done? Is it a vice in that I am hopelessly addicted to it and am a complete emotional and cognitive mess without it? Is my penchant for perseverating on possibilities far into the future a good thing, preparing me to jump at decisions when I need to make them? Is it a bad thing, taking me away from the present moment and draining my emotional energy?

The answer to all of these questions seems to be yes. I am only beginning to understand the interconnectedness between my best self and my worst flaws.

Every Virtue, Taken to Its Logical Conclusion, Becomes a Vice

We are all an orchestra of traits, often beautiful when they play together in harmony. But allow one trait to dominate, and it can crowd out the music and just produce noise.

I work best when organized. When I have a good action plan that outlines what has been done by when and by whom, I am in the zone. And this makes me a good team leader. I know how to provide the systems and tools to organize a group of people toward a common outcome. I know how to keep us all on track.

But when things are moving quickly and balls start getting dropped, I have a hard time knowing when to keep running and when to stop and pick up the balls. When things devolve into disorganization, I get frustrated and have a hard time keeping my team focused on the right things. I want to just hit stop and clean up the mess. But the problem is that sometimes hitting stop to clean up the mess keeps us from getting where we want to go.

The last few weeks of my campaign for public office in 2012 were a shit show. People I had been trying to get to pay attention to my race—donors, volunteers, media, voters—started paying attention seemingly all at once. I went from "Why won't people return my calls?" to "Why are so many people calling to tell me what I should be doing?" Soon I began wondering if we were doing everything we needed to be doing. Had we called back every prospective donor? Had we knocked on every door in our field plan? Had the team and I responded to every important email? I began waking up at three forty-five in the morning to organize to-do lists and comb through emails to see if everything was getting done.

This was the wrong instinct. At a time when I should have been most focused, I was distracted by fears that we were not organized enough and sleeping even less than a candidate should to try to stay organized. When I should have been inspiring others, knocking on every door that I could, calling every voter I could reach, I was tired and stressed, trying to operate in a system moving faster than my organizational structures could support.

So I had to let go. I saw into the future and realized if I kept trying to be the candidate and the chief operating officer of the campaign, I would wear myself out and burn my team out. And no voter wants to vote for a tired, snippy, cranky candidate. I had to accept the imperfections. I had to embrace our failures. And I had to move forward staying laser-focused on our message and our campaign's belief in the potential for a brighter future for our community.

Our virtues, extended to their logical if absurd conclusions, become vices. Humility can devolve into a failure to acknowledge and bring forth one's true talents. Confidence can become arrogance. Commitment to collaboration can morph into focusing on comforting a team above working on the urgent needs of the community we serve. Discipline and hard work can become such a singular focus that we fail to see and grab new opportunities as they arise.

The thing is we all love our virtues. After all, they are what have made us successful to date. The hard thing to see, and even harder to accept, is that what has made us good at what we do isn't necessarily what will make us great moving forward.

The trick is to acknowledge and accept that even our virtues have limitations. The goal is not to become so committed to a virtue, or a practice of virtue, that we crowd out other complementary virtues. We must be cautious about holding on to our best virtues so fiercely that we ignore when our own extreme adherence to them becomes an obsession rather than a strength. We need to know when to let go of justice and claim mercy, when to leave behind discipline and embrace spontaneity, when to drop critical thinking and pick up hope.

At the Heart of Every Vice Lies a Virtue

But here's the thing. If every virtue extended to its logical conclusion becomes a vice, then something good lies deep within each vice.

I beat myself up over my vices. When I oversleep, I am frustrated by my laziness. When I overindulge, I am ashamed of my gluttony. When I go for the jugular in an argument, I am dismayed by my inability to control my own hotheadedness.

Once, early on in my tenure running schools in Los Angeles, a bank rep called to let me know that I needed to come into the branch to resolve some minor administrative issue. I was immediately fit to be tied. I went off on the guy. I ranted about how I shouldn't have to take time away from running my schools to come to the bank to deal with some administrative matter. The poor bank rep just kept apologizing and affirming what I was saying but telling me it was the only way he could resolve the issue. Finally, furious beyond measure that I had to stop my work and leave campus to come in, I raised my voice: "This is bad for kids, you know. Tell me you know this is bad for kids, and I'll come in." "This is bad for kids," he replied meekly, and I agreed to come in shortly.

Reading this, you might be thinking, *What a jerk*. And writing this, I am definitely thinking, *What a jerk*. At that moment, though, caught up in work I knew was deeply important, I resented—with a proportionality not merited by the circumstances—being told I had to focus on what I thought was a trivial matter. I can be a real asshole sometimes. This behavior can be uncalled for, unkind, and unfairly directed at good people. I am ashamed of this.

But shame does little to make us better. Whether it's shame over inactivity, overindulgences, or bouts of unkindness—the three things I most often deride myself for—the story that these vices are deviant character flaws doesn't help me want to address them head on. Instead, I shy away from dealing with them, convinced that they are bugs in my system. And when I do, the story I tell myself about these flaws holds me back from being bold and courageous in taking on big challenges because I fear I am too flawed to rise to the occasion.

What I have begun to uncover, though, is a more compelling—and arguably truer—story of these vices. At the core of many of these harmful and toxic behaviors lies a nugget of goodness. For me, it has become more helpful in wrestling with these weaknesses of spirit to see them as virtues spun out of control, not as fundamental problems with my being. Not for the sake of spin but for the sake of starting in a more honest and productive place than shame.

Buried beneath my instinct to yell at the bank rep was a deep care for and commitment to my students and school community. I resented being pulled away from that work for a trivial matter. That commitment to my students spun out of control. It crowded out care for the bank rep, an openness toward creative problem-solving, and a groundedness that would have allowed me—and not my circumstances—to determine my reactions.

When I am inefficient in tackling the work at hand, when I check social media and daydream and put off hard important tasks for easy trivial tasks, my mind is telling me that it needs rest in order to tackle hard things. There are better ways of giving it rest than procrastination and delay, but the core is good. When I overeat or overdrink and wake up the next day sluggish, I now try to acknowledge that it was a desire to celebrate the blessings of good food and drink, often in the company of good people, that I got a little carried away. Just like the virtues we saw before can be taken to extremes and cause real harm, so my vices worked backward have a kernel of goodness at their core.

If at the heart of *our* vices beats some deep goodness, then that's also the case for others. I am not talking about toxic vices that dole out harm. There is no goodness at the heart of abuse. I am instead confronting the everyday vices of our imperfections. In my days leading a team of community organizers, we often faced the challenge of getting new organizers out in the community to meet with people. We trained them on how to do a one-on-one meeting, to share their story and begin to build a relationship with community leaders. We would practice over and over again. And then, when they would be told to schedule twenty-five to thirty meetings a week, they would often begin to stall. They would schedule five meetings the first week, then ten meetings the next, but go down to seven meetings after that.

When I would talk with them to try to understand why they weren't scheduling more meetings, it would often become clear that they were paralyzed by fear of doing the meetings wrong. They were worried they would be awkward, or fail to build a relationship, or somehow just do the meeting wrong.

At the heart of this procrastination was perfectionism. These young organizers were hired because they had successfully tackled so much in their lives. But community organizing is different, messy. It takes a lot of practice and the honing of good instincts to get halfway decent at it.

But fear of failing stops you from doing the work you need to do to get better at it. Remember Anne Lamott's quote, "Perfectionism is the voice of the oppressor"? It stops good people from starting important work. I knew that the new organizers had a strong and deep drive to do well, so when I saw this procrastination, I knew it was not laziness or a lack of commitment to the work but instead a perverted perfectionism. In trying to create the environment for our people to succeed, I said, "Your first fifty one-on-one meetings will be terrible. So get through them as quickly as possible while everyone knows you're still new at this." Seeing the goodness in the flaws does not excuse bad behavior. It's not a "get out of jail free" card. Instead, an honest assessment of the interconnectedness of our virtues and vices gives me—and others—the fortitude to square our shoulders and face down our vices directly and calmly. But perhaps more importantly, seeing the link between virtue and vice gives us the touch of grace we often need to deal with others. When colleagues drop the ball, when allies bully, when community leaders fail to stand up for what is right, we might still get frustrated, even angry. But instead of writing these people off as obstacles to justice, we can try to look for the virtue hidden in the vice. When we find it, we are more able to remind ourselves that the person standing in our way might be someone who can be worked with and not just an opponent to be bested.

Walt Whitman reminds us that "we contain multitudes." And we are indeed complex creatures full of those multitudes, including contradictions. I am a collection of selves swimming about in a maelstrom I call "Brian." I am kind and impatient, curious and single-minded. Which self will rise and greet the moment is often a mystery.

While this is true, something simpler is also true. Our virtues and vices are not just competing polarities. They are fruits of the same seeds.

So don't lean into your shame and don't fetishize your virtues. Virtues have their roles, but they also have their limits. They have made you successful at what you've done to date. But to paraphrase Marshall Goldsmith, what got you here won't always get you there. Learn to loosen your grasp, even if just once in a while, on your favorite virtues when they are not suited to the moment. This doesn't mean abandoning who you are and what makes you great.

It means widening the aperture just a bit to look around at your other strengths to see what else may be of use.

I also invite you to soften your criticism of the vices in yourself and in others. Remember they are often our goodness gone awry. When you can see your own shortcomings as misguided virtues, you give yourself the room to change more wholeheartedly, without the heavy burdens of shame or defensiveness. And when you see the faults in others as their virtues contorted in the moment, you can hold space for them in your work instead of casting them out or turning them into enemies.

Accepting the limits of your virtues and the source of goodness in your vices, imagine what goodness you could unleash on the world.

11

Our Journey Stories

I woke up on my thirty-fifth birthday unemployed, single, and looking ahead to spending most of the day alone.

Three weeks earlier, I had conceded defeat in my campaign to serve in the California State Assembly, having fallen thirty-one votes short out of forty-two thousand cast. The transition from the cacophony of one of the most contentious elections in the state to utter silence was swift and stark. For months, I woke up each day at 4:00 a.m. to email, knocked on hundreds of doors, made dozens of phone calls, worked with scores of volunteers, and crashed into bed at 10:00 p.m. I had poured everything into the campaign—forgoing much of a personal life or even a dating life. Now the campaign was over, and I had little to show for it. All in all, if you had asked my twenty-two-year-old self what I wanted my life to be like on my thirty-fifth birthday, this was not it.

Over the next few months, I bounced back. Slowly. Two months after that birthday, I started a new job I loved. A few months after that, I met the man who would become my husband and the father of my daughter. But this story is not about the rebound. It is about what I learned in that lonely, quiet place nursing a public failure and staring into an uncertain future.

Going into the campaign, the greatest fear I faced was the shame of falling flat on my face in public. I worried that I wouldn't be able to rally the volunteers or the donations; I was able to do that. I worried that I would make stupid mistakes on the campaign trail; at least my mistakes were not embarrassing. I worried that I would come up short, and all my supporters and opponents and even the observers would find me wanting; if they did, I didn't hear about it.

In the end, I did the best job I could. I left nothing on the field. It's not that I ran a perfect campaign. In hindsight, I see realities and contexts that were obscured from me in the scrum of a competitive race. But I know I made the best decisions I knew how to make with the information I had at the time. So I wasn't coming off the campaign steeped in shame or regret.

But I did come off the campaign feeling . . . lost. For nearly two years, I had been telling everyone around me a story—a journey story. It was a story about who I was and what I was going to do over the next decade in elected office. I told donors this story and volunteers this story. I told voters this story. I even told myself this story.

And then one day, that story dissipated. It wasn't a slow evaporation. It dried up immediately, the day after the campaign ended. I could no longer see the way forward. I was in professional vertigo. I didn't know if I was moving forward in my career or backward or even standing still. I went through the motions and did work I cared about, but I wasn't sure where I was headed.

It was in this period that I realized that throughout the campaign, and even leading up to it, I had become addicted to my journey story. Eventually, this story was all I thought about. It permeated every part of my life. I let it define me. It is not that I was confident I would win. It's just that I didn't build out the mental space to consider a plan B, which was probably for the best; I don't think great candidates spend their energy thinking about what to do if they lose.

But as hectic and nerve-wracking as the campaign was, the story gave me direction and meaning. It spurred me on. It enabled me to rally others to my side. And when it was gone with no replacement, I felt lost and unnerved and confused. Only in its absence did I realize how strong the journey story was, and how it had served as a central scaffolding to my sense of purpose. So when I woke up on my thirty-fifth birthday, I felt mired in loss, not immersed in gratitude for my life to date.

We are all held together by story. It is evolutionary. Jonathan Gottschall tells us, "We are as a species addicted to story. Even when the body goes to sleep, the mind stays up all night telling itself stories."

But what does *story* really mean? When we hear the word, we throw it into the same pot as myth, fiction, legend, even lie. We laugh at our silly ancestors who believed in mountaintop gods and their thunderbolts. We clench our teeth in frustration at our fellow citizens who believe in the tweeted lies or conspiracy theories that come from the stories they create. Stories are fictions, maybe untruths, we often tell ourselves, and many of us work to abandon them on the path toward self-actualization.

But there is another meaning of *story*. There is story as narrative structure to our lives. Story as the conceptual skeleton that gives form to our everyday actions and emotions and experiences. Truth or falsity is not the most relevant part of our stories. The defining element of our story is how well it gives shape to our lives.

And that frame, the journey story, is a particular story about where we are headed. These stories can be big or small. They can describe a multiyear path ahead. Or they can tell what the next few weeks will look like on a project. Maybe it's a story that we are working to abolish prisons. Or maybe it's a story that we are making our jobs safe for all workers. Or maybe it's a story that we are raising healthy children who will marry and secure good jobs.

A journey story is not the only story we tell ourselves. Our journey stories intersect with other stories. Our story of self describes how our history, our values, our talents, and our loved ones all weave together to unveil our central identity. A conflict story tells what enemies we face along the way. But at the heart, the journey story is the story of what path we are on and where we are headed.

Journey stories are important, essential for three reasons. First, they ground us. In a world of uncertainty and complexity, it can be daunting to make sense of everything around us. We can lose the forest for the trees. We can struggle to process new information. But a journey story fixes us to the path. It gives us a frame of reference to interpret what is going on around us. It helps us tune out extraneous information. It slows our breathing and focuses our vision, so to speak, and helps us to move forward confidently and clearly.

Second, they inspire us. It can be difficult to wake up every day and do the work. The days are often long, and the nights can be filled with worry. We can easily grow weary. But a journey story gives us hope. It paints a world that is more beautiful than the one we live in now and connects our everyday drudgery to that vibrant future world. It gives us the energy and rationale to wake up each day and do the hard work.

Finally, they draw us together with allies. With a common journey story, our families or our teams can all work together more seamlessly. Think of yourself on a boat with those working with you. Without a common journey story, you might all be rowing in a different direction, ultimately going nowhere. But with a shared journey story, you can begin to move in the same direction. If you and your co-parent know you are working to get your daughters into a good college, you can split homework duties and jointly save for college tuition. If you and other parent volunteers know you are working to raise enough money for the PTA so that the school can buy more computers, then you can collaborate to put on the school fundraiser.

In short, journey stories are powerful guides showing us how to treat ourselves and how to approach others.

But when we allow the stories of where we are headed to become a central font of meaning in our lives—and not simply tools we use to move us forward—they begin to hold a power over us that is undeserved and unproductive. When our journey story supplants the more essential stories in our lives—our story of self, our story of our family or community, our story of our values—we run the risk of becoming lost when our journey story changes or falls apart. We are so much stronger when we hold fast to our deeper stories and grasp lightly the stories of where our path is taking us.

As I write this chapter, we are months into a brutal pandemic. I am at home. I am always at home these days, sheltering in place 140 miles from my city office. My coworkers are all doing versions of the same.

When I think back over a year ago, I think of all the plans we had as a team and as an organization. We were in the middle of a five-year strategic plan that laid out the impact we would have over the period. We had concrete goals and a firm budget for the year. And then, in a few-week period, everything we envisioned went up in smoke. We had no community events or fundraisers. Our legislative actions ground to a halt in the face of a state legislature that wasn't meeting. As everything we were working toward dissipated, we stared out into a spring and early summer and saw nothing.

Because of my experience after the campaign, of recognizing the journey story for what it is and letting it go when it no longer served me, I was able to see more clearly what was happening than I otherwise may have. I was reminded that everything we were working toward—all our plans and ideas and budgets—were just guiding stories. They weren't certainties or realities. They were stories we believed in, stories we told ourselves so that we could get up every day and do the work. And these stories were critically important. They gave us a sense of purpose and direction. They spurred us forward. They enabled us to rally others—our donors, our volunteers, our community leaders—to join with us to make a difference. But nonetheless, they were simply stories. And they no longer served us, so we needed to readily let them go so we could focus first on our deeper, truer stories: The story of our deep love for our LGBTQ+ community. The story of our resilience in the face of resistance and plague. Grounded in those more fundamental stories, we could eventually create a new journey story for our team that would rally us and our community toward a new path forward. And we did. We created new programs to meet the needs of those most vulnerable. We set new goals and revised old budgets to allow us to respond in the moment to our community's evolving needs. We let go of the old journey stories so we could readily grab on to new ones.

Just like me on the campaign or my team on the cusp of the pandemic, you, too, are undoubtedly in the middle of your own journey story right now. The story of what type of activist you will become. The story of what job you are working toward. The story of how high your career will take you and how broad and deep your life's impact will be. This story is undoubtedly useful but might not be robust enough to hold a full and evolving life.

Maybe we all shouldn't cling so tightly to these stories of where we are headed. Obsess over them. Worry about losing them. No matter what we tell ourselves, the path ahead is always uncertain and unknown. In the end, we should use our journey stories but not let them drive us. Use them as tools to push you forward and help inform your hard choices. But don't allow them to define who you think you are. When things change—and they will change—loosen your hold on your former story a little bit or open up the journey of the story to hold something wider, changing, growing. Even if these reins fall slack and you don't yet have a grasp of some new story to hold on to, you will. After all, we are people of story. Our ancestors have created stories for millennia. If history is any guide, you likely won't be without a journey story for long. So honor your journey stories and acknowledge their importance. Draft toward them when they are helpful and work to evolve them when their old tropes don't work. But know they exist to serve us; we do not live to serve them. They offer no more constraints than we allow them to. They offer no more certainty than the world ever provides. And in those moments when you need to let go of an old journey story and find a new evolving one to grab on to, I hope you remind yourself of your deeper stories and hold yourself gently as you reach confidently into the unknown.

12

Make Room for Joy

Once early in my job running the nonprofit in LA, I went to the then-new and still-beautiful Walt Disney Concert Hall a few blocks from my office. Before seeing that temple to music, I didn't know steel could ripple or metal could flow. But what architect Frank Gehry had created was a revelation—a structure that manifested the lightness and fluidity of music itself.

In the entrance hall, I saw the listing of the city's wealthiest people, institutions, and businesses heralded for their benevolence, a celebration of the millions they had invested to birth this building.

I seethed. Into that cathedral to music—only blocks from one of the largest homeless encampments in America, a mile from the Rodney King uprisings, less than five miles from the heart of gang violence in East LA—the wealthy poured their generosity and accepted their praise. They then literally turned their backs on the epidemic of poverty and racial injustice they profited from and drove to their gated homes with manicured lawns fed with diverted water. Some of these same names were ones I couldn't get to consider or support my teachers' work in overburdened schools. But here they stumbled over each other to erect this monument to their generosity.

In my anger, I not only resented them; I resented the arts and music. I thought about all the museums and concert halls heralding the names of the wealthy and saw these efforts as frivolous distractions that made society comfortable and self-satisfied instead of sharpening our focus on attacking injustice and eliminating inequity.

But as the waves of anger ebbed, I realized I was wrong in that moment. Not in my frustration at the charitable people who prioritized giving that secured them praise over giving that tackled our deepest social ills. I was wrong in my view that the arts were wasteful indulgences.

I love story and art. I pile books throughout my home and revel in live music. I love art that pops with color and movies that reveal deep questions. The marks of human civilization aren't merely scientific advancements or technical marvels. They are just as much the creative endeavors that inspire and give light to their world: the amphitheaters of ancient Greece, the Han dynasty poets, the Lascaux murals. These are not diversions from human advancement. They are essential expressions of our collective spirit.

Because what we have known since our ancient forebearers first put crude paint to rough walls is that joy is essential to our existence. We cannot cleave that which inspires and moves and elates from the central definition of our identity. When we dance with abandon and eat great food and drink good wine, we are not turning our backs to the more essential parts of who we are; we are embracing a coequal part of our nature. When we celebrate each other and the art we create, we aren't necessarily shirking our duty to lighten the load of those oppressed; we are honoring the fullness of who we are. For the functional and joyful intertwine as dual helices of our being. We are both duty and joy. Denying joy—even for the lofty aims of advancing justice—denies a part of who we are.

The work is hard. The struggle goes on with no end in sight. Those who are poor will always be with us, at least in our lifetime. For those of us attuned enough to injustice to work on its eradication, the world will feed us a constant loop. We cannot unsee what we have seen.

Once we realize the pain of poverty, the tragedy of illness, and the cruelties of violence, it can be hard to turn our backs on them. We run the risk of having the world slowly crush us under the weight of the enormity of its problems and the expectations we lay on ourselves to remedy them.

And yet we are afforded countless tiny moments along the way to appreciate the goodness around us. Maybe it is the song on the radio, or the company of our friends, or the sweet smells of home cooking. It is not selfish to stop and take those in. It is not an indulgence to rest from our work and dance and sing with family and friends. By doing so, we claim the other parts of our essence. By doing so, we embrace the fullness of our being.

One cold February evening in Chicago, I joined a hundred other people to huddle into a cozy bar to hear LGBTQ+ people step up to the mic and tell personal stories. I was there to see my friend Jackie, who mesmerized the audience by talking about queer magic. She regaled us with stories of her and her friends dancing in a crowded club, glittered up and laughing. In the face of a world that wanted to deny their existence, they claimed their space and celebrated in the love of each other. Our ability as queer people to laugh, and dance, and hold joy in bodies and relationships the dominant culture often wants to punish is magic. Pride in the face of those who want us to be ashamed is our superpower. We can and should fight to demand that our dignity be acknowledged and that laws protect us. But when queer people dance and march and sing, we are also performing our duty to be fully authentic in a world that wants to quash that authenticity.

Just as justice is our calling, so is joy. By taking time to celebrate the little things—and sometimes the big things—that bring light to the world, we honor the wholeness of the world. We refuse to allow our communities to be defined merely by their faults and tragedies. In this, we remember we are fighting not simply for the elimination of pain. We are fighting to claim our community's wholeness. We are fighting for our own wholeness.

I am not sure I would have truly seen the importance of joy in activism without the lessons that parenting my daughter, Joey, has brought me. Perhaps all parents feel this way. Or maybe it is more acutely held by those of us who are queer activists, those of us who fight for justice and come home to the blessing of families we know we were not always guaranteed. Or maybe it is the unique contours of Joey's life that have brought forth the truth of joy in such stark and vibrant relief.

The diagnosis stalked us for two years before it stepped into the light one warm March morning.

"Dads, I hate calling it *cerebral palsy [CP]*," our daughter's pediatric neurologist told us on the phone, "because it sends parents down a spiral, picturing the most severe cases. But Josephine has a mild form of spastic hemiplegia, a condition under the broader umbrella of CP."

We knew this was the most likely outcome of the call. Joey had a strong preference to use her left hand as early as six months old, years before children typically develop a hand preference. She didn't sit up on her own until she was thirteen months old, nearly six months after children usually do. She didn't walk on her own until shortly after her second birthday, a year later than most. Joey is curious about everyone and everything around her. She talks nearly incessantly from the moment she wakes up. Car rides with her are a perpetual recitation of whom she played with in daycare, demands for certain songs, and a chorus of "Hey, Papa, what's that?" But even at nearly three years old, she isn't a solid walker, and she refuses to use her right hand for almost any activity, big or small.

For most of the past two years, we had been in active "wait and see" mode. She has been in weekly physical therapy and occupational therapy, she went through a bout of ankle braces, and she has seen an array of specialists. But there could be many things accounting for her developmental delays, and a CP diagnosis is not so much a clear *a-ha* resulting from a single test as much as it is a collection of clues neurologists gather to make an informed diagnosis. CP is a form of brain damage caused in utero or during or immediately following birth. Often it is the result of a fetus having a ministroke that leaves behind some brain damage. A diagnosis requires an MRI, which at Joey's age was a more significant procedure requiring her to undergo general anesthesia. Any resulting diagnosis wouldn't have changed what we were currently doing— PT, OT, bracing. So for months, we continued our work with her and waited to see any impact of the interventions.

But as we were approaching her third birthday, Josephine still remained delayed. We decided it was time to get the MRI. If it was CP, having a confirmed diagnosis would help us access the battery of services she would need as she approached school age. The day we walked her into the Children's Hospital in Chicago, Joey ambled down the hallways talking to every person she saw, asking them their name. Watching strangers melt as they interact with Josephine is a regular part of our role as parents.

A week later, and sure enough, her neurologist shared that Joey had scarring on the left side of her brain, indicating she likely had had a stroke as a fetus. The result is that the muscles on the right side of her body are harder for her to use than those on the left. Joey will need to spend a lifetime working to strengthen and loosen the muscles in her right leg and in her right arm and hand. "She might not be an Olympic figure skater," her neurologist told us, "but she can live a very full and active life." Spastic hemiplegia, her form of CP, won't get worse neurologically as she ages. But she—and we—will have to work diligently to keep those muscles on her right side strong and loose so they don't stiffen and contract over time.

I don't know much as a parent, but I do know that from the moment your child comes into your life, the thought of them hurting becomes one of your biggest fears. Over a year ago, when the possibility that Joey might have a lifelong neurological condition first crossed my mind, I sat in the rocking chair on our front porch and cried. WebMD searches and YouTube videos and a lifetime of images of people living with disabilities merged in my mind to form a movie of struggle and ostracization and pain for Joey. I didn't want life for my little girl to be any harder, any meaner, or any crueler than it had to be.

And then, in a moment, an echo of my own parents' concerns for me as a young man rang softly. I came out to my father on a ride to the hardware store one Saturday morning in 2001 when I was twenty-four years old. My dad told me he loved me but that he was worried for me. He didn't want me to be limited in my career, to end up alone, or to be harmed. This was the time when discrimination against gay people in the workplace was perfectly legal and when civil unions, let alone marriages, weren't even possible. This was shortly after Matthew Shepherd had been brutally murdered. My father's fear for my struggle and ostracization and pain was palpable.

But what he couldn't see then—and to be honest, what I couldn't see then—is that my being gay would lead to the greatest joys in my life. It has served as the foundation for my current career as an LGBTQ+ civil rights leader, work that gives me great meaning and purpose. It has led me to my husband and to the beautiful life we have built together. It has brought me my daughter, whom I love with a fierceness and softness I didn't know possible. These joys are in my life not in spite of my being gay. They are in my life because of my being gay. But at the time of my coming out, when the future seemed bleak and uncertain, this joy was not visible to me or my parents.

This is how oppressive systems work, be they homophobia or ableism. They mark the conditions that separate us from the dominant groups in society as struggles. They wrap our differences in shame. They whisper to us that our lives will be mere shadows of the fulfilling life experiences those in the more powerful social groups will build. These are the lies they tell to reinforce their own power.

I have so much to learn to serve as Joey's best advocate and champion. It will take an incredible amount of curiosity and humility to get up to speed. But what I have learned—what I know now—is to make room for the joy. My husband and I sat on our couch the week before the MRI, and over bourbons, we began making meaning of what may lie ahead. I shared with him my recognition that decades ago my parents, our parents, sat in a similar place of worry for very different reasons. He nodded.

So we began bouncing off joyful possibilities. Maybe it is through the network of people living with CP that Joey meets the love of her life. Maybe it is her spastic hemiplegia that inspires her to become an artist or author giving voice to her experience. Maybe it is her time in the care of her loving and competent medical team that fuels her to become a doctor or a nurse or a therapist. At a time when the world would point us to fear and sadness, we held vigil for joy.

I don't mean to be Pollyanna here. I know that Joey will face real challenges. The adults we've come across with CP talk about frustrations dealing with their own body's limitations, the hurt of being shunned by their peers, the physical pain. But the world does a good enough job on its own of reminding us of the struggle. It doesn't need us to pile on, for Joey or for ourselves.

I also know analogies are rough. Hew too closely to the comparison and you sand off the unique contours of either the queer experience or the CP experience. To be blunt, having CP is not the same as being gay. There will be times when Joey's pain matches my own, and I will show her my scars to teach her that we hurt and heal and get stronger. There will also be times when her struggle is distinct from mine, and I will simply have to sit and hold space with her.

But for now, the most powerful and subversive thing I can do is carve out room for joy. Later, I can draw from my own experiences as a member of a marginalized community to model for her how to stare down shame and pity. Find your people. Surround yourself with chosen community. Learn your history. Demand full inclusion. And, beyond all else, celebrate. Dance in your homes and gather in the streets.

The late Ruth Bader Ginsburg taught us, "So often in life, things that you regard as an impediment turn out to be great good fortune." I don't know how the karmic scales will balance triumph and defeat in Joey's life. But I know the universe rarely gives with one hand. It doles out both pain and blessings. In light of this, my husband and I have decided to model what we have learned. As a gift to our daughter, who has enriched our lives in unimaginable ways and who has filled our hearts with deep abiding love, we will invite grace in. We will hold space for the full range of happy possibilities that may unfold. We will make room for joy.

Among the many lessons being Joey's papa has taught me is that this making room for joy should not stop when I cross the threshold of my home each day and enter the world of my work. I should—and I do—work hard to build LGBTQ+ power, to fight on behalf of queer families, and to agitate for pro-equality laws. But I am also intentional about holding fast to the parts of my life and my work that make my heart sing and my soul lighten. I celebrate the team I work in solidarity with. I watch good TV and read great books. I carve out time to run and spend quiet time alone in nature. I play with my daughter and eat meals with my husband. These regular bits of joy are not ancillary components of my life to be grabbed at whenever a gap in my schedule opens up. They are essential parts of who I am. They must be sought after, guarded, and allowed to flourish. Thanks in large part to the gift of my daughter in my life, I have now learned to approach these moments that unleash joy with the same commitment and reverence as I use in meeting the day-to-day tasks required to fight for justice. Doing so makes me a more complete and authentic activist. Doing so makes me more fully human.

You know which pain calls to you for relief. You know which injustice fires you up. You know which inequity enrages you. But just as important as it is to turn your mind and heart to the wrongs of the world, it is equally important to cultivate your sense of joy and wonder. To know what captures your eye with delight. To know what binds you tightly to others in warm affinity. To know what makes you tilt your head back and laugh and move your body with abandon.

May you find your calling and leap. May you seek first to understand. May you approach the work with care for—but not obsession with—the outcomes. But if you take nothing else from these field notes, this is what I ask of you. Find the blessings in the ordinary. Yes, I hope you work to make your corner of the world a fairer and more vibrant place. But at the beginning of each day, and also at its end, and many times throughout, I hope you notice and lift up the day's beauty.

And turn this commitment outward to your community as well. Deny injustice the right to define the story. Tell our tragedies that they will not form our identities. When violence threatens to define the victim's life, hold fast to their laughter. When illness attempts to claim the patient's identity, celebrate their talents and humor. When poverty tries to describe a community only by what it lacks, tell the story of its wealth.

In all that you do, lift up joy and bring forth beauty from the wings. Let your simple goodness and the everyday goodness of the world around you claim center stage. For you, in all your imperfections and wonder, are unparalleled in this world. Every time you hold even the smallest space for joy, you shine and bring light and color to the world.

So make room for joy and shine.

Acknowledgments

What you see on these pages is only possible because of countless coconspirators, teachers, champions, and loved ones. I hope you have noticed the deep gratitude I hold for them in the stories and lessons I have shared. Some though, deserve a special shout out for the work they did to bring this book to life. To Giles Anderson and Lil Copan who once again believed in the possibility of a book—authentically told and vulnerably shared. Thank you for shepherding an idea into the world with such care and fierceness. To Jessica Cordova Kramer, Jim LoBianco,

Katharine Strunk, Mony Ruiz-Velasco, Mercedes Kane, and Claudia Love Mair who trusted me with their criticisms so I could hone the message. And finally, to Toby Eveland, who gives me the space, the love, and the encouragement to tell my stories, and sometimes our stories, to the world. I am braver and stronger because of you.

Notes

Chapter 1

Let me start: Wanjiru Kibera, "Between A Rock and A Hard Place," *The Moth*, Recorded May 28, 2018; Original Air Date April 30, 2019.

Chapter 2

Elizabeth Gilbert tells us: Elizabeth Gilbert, *Eat Pray Love*, Riverhead Books, New York, 2010.

Maybe another way: Frederick Buechner, *Wishful Thinking*, Harper-One, New York, 1993.

The author Anne Lamott: Anne Lamott, *Bird By Bird: Some Instructions on Writing and Life*, Knopf Doubleday, New York, 1995.

The Jesuit Priest: Krista Tippett, host, "The Calling of Delight: Gangs, Service, and Kinship," *On Being with Krista Tippett*, February 26, 2013.

So write that: Lamott, *Bird By Bird*.

But for many of us: Elizabeth Gilbert, *Big Magic: Creative Living Beyond Fear*, Bloomsburg Publishing, New York, 2016.

Or of Noreen Riols: Noreen Riols, "The Spy Who Loved Me," *The Moth Radio Hour*, February 2015.

The Roman philosopher Seneca taught us: Seneca, Letter 78, *Moral Letters to Lucilius*.

First, as Brené Brown teaches: Krista Tippett, host, "Courage Is Born from Struggle," *On Being with Krista Tippett*, March 18, 2016.

Once again, Brené Brown: Tippett, "Courage Is Born from Struggle."

"If you are on your own path": Joseph Campbell, *Reflections on the Art of Living: A Joseph Campbell Companion*, ed. Diane K. Olson, Harper Perennial, New York, 1995.

"Have hope, not expectations": Beginnings and Endings, *Dark*, written by Baran bo Obdar, Jantje Friese, and Ronny Schalk, Season 2, Episode 1, Netflix, 2019.

As the poet Reverend Victoria Safford: Victoria Safford, "The Gates of Hope," *Stanford Social Innovation Review*, August 19, 2015.

As Father Greg Boyle: Krista Tippett, host, "The Calling of Delight: Gangs, Service, and Kinship." *On Being with Krista Tippett*, February 26, 2013.

Chapter 3

Krishna tells Arjuna: Stephen Mitchell, *The Bhagavad Gita*, Crown Publications, New York, 2002.

Locked in a jail in Birmingham: Martin Luther King, Jr., Letter from a Birmingham City Jail, *The Atlantic Monthly*, August 1963, The Negro Is Your Brother, Vol. 212, No. 2.

"I've been there": Nina Simone, *Mississippi Goddamn*.

The Gita may tell us: Mohandas K. Gandhi, *The Bhagavad Gita According to Gandhi*, North Atlantic Books, Berkeley, 2009.

He who broods over results: Gandhi, *The Bhagavad Gita According to Gandhi*.

The waste of emotional energy: Annie Dillard, *Pilgrim at Tinker Creek* (1st U.S. ed.), Harper's Magazine Press, New York, 1974.

When he coaches: Louis Chew, "Nick Saban: Do Your Job and Trust the Process," *Constant Renewal*, June 2, 2018.

Henri Nouwen, the great: Henri Nouwen, *Our Greatest Gift*, HarperOne, New York, September 22, 2009.

Chapter 4

Over time, walls that: Leonard Cohen, *Anthem*.

And then looking at it: Marius von Senden, *Space and Sight: There Perception of Space and Shape in the Congenitally Blind Before and After Operation*, translated by Peter Heath, The Free Press, Glencoe, IL, 1960.

Chapter 5

Philosopher Kwame Anthony Appiah: Krista Tippett, host, "Sidling Up to Difference: Social Change and Moral Revolutions," *On Being with Krista Tippett*, March 24, 2011.

He said, 'You're my son's': "Kwame Anthony Appiah—Sidling Up to Difference: Social Change and Moral Revolutions," *The On Being Project*, March 24, 2011.

You talk about soccer: "Kwame Anthony Appiah—Sidling Up to Difference."

Claudia Rankine, the American poet: Krista Tippett, host, "How Can I Say This So We Can Stay in This Car Together?" *On Being with Krista Tippett*, January 10, 2019.

Greg Boyle once said: Greg Boyle, *Barking to the Choir: The Power of Radical Kinship*, Simon & Shuster, New York, 2017, p. 6.

Chapter 7

As civil rights activist: Brittany Packnett Cunningham, *Twitter*, October 11, 2017.

Anne Lamott stares down: Anne Lamott, *Bird By Bird*, Pantheon Books, New York, 1994.

Or as Brené Brown: Brené Brown, "Why Your Critics Aren't the Ones Who Count," Talk at 99U A Behance Conference, December 4, 2013.

This is what comedian: Amy Poehler, *Yes Please*, Picador, New York, January 1, 2015.

Remember Frederick Buechner's: Frederick Buechner, *Wishful Thinking*, HarperOne, New York, 1993.

"Lighthouses": Anne Lamott, *Bird By Bird*, Pantheon Books, New York, 1994.

Maybe we could: John Steinbeck, *East of Eden*, Penguin Classics, New York, January 1, 1952.

Chapter 8

"I have almost reached": Martin Luther King, Jr., Letter from a Birmingham City Jail, *The Atlantic Monthly*, August 1963, The Negro Is Your Brother, Vol. 212, No. 2.

The activist sent an open letter: Benji Hart, "Happening Now: Trans-Led Coalition Shuts Down Chicago Pride Parade," *Radical Faggot*, June 25, 2017.

The vegan professor and activist: Melanie Joy, "The Green Pill with Dr. Melanie Joy," *The Ezra Klein Show*, June 11, 2018.

"Be sure you put your feet": Commonly attributed to Abraham Lincoln.

This is about the producer: Her original letter was posted to her Tumblr account and is quoted at Peter Helman, "Read Taylor Swift's Open Letter to Apple Music," *Stereogum*, June 21, 2015.

The god Krishna instructs: Stephen Mitchell, *The Bhagavad Gita*, Crown Publications, New York, 2002.

"Nature is never in peace,": Krista Tippett, host, "The Alchemy of Pilgrimage," *On Being with Krista Tippett*, August 14, 2014.

Chapter 9

Annie Dillard tells us: Annie Dillard, *Pilgrim at Tinker Creek* (1st U.S. ed.), Harper's Magazine Press, New York, 1974.

Chapter 10

Walt Whitman reminds us: Walt Whitman, "Song of Myself, 51."

Chapter 11

Jonathan Gottschall tells: Jonathan Gottschall, *The Storytelling Animal: How Stories Make Us Human*, Mariner Books, New York, 2013.

Chapter 12

"Dads, I hate calling it": An original version of this essay appeared in Brian C. Johnson, "A Daughter's Diagnosis and a Refusal to Give in to Despair," *The Advocate*, May 12, 2021.

The late Ruth Bader Ginsburg taught us: Referenced in Tamar Lapin, "Some of Ruth Bader Ginsburg's Most Memorable Quotes," *New York Post*, September 18, 2020.